Leadership Evo

A practical guide for redefining leadership in your organization and unlocking your highest potential

Jody N Holland

Foreword by Stephan Schiffman

ISBN: 978-0-9839835-2-1

ISBN-13: 978-0-9839835-2-1

DEDICATION

This book is dedicated to all the leaders in this world that embrace the reality that leadership is truly about influence. It is dedicated to the leaders who are willing to step up and challenge what they think about leadership and management, who are dedicated to unlocking an organization's highest potential.

CONTENTS

ACKNOWLEDGMENTS

I would like to say a special thank you to the great leaders that helped to make this book possible.

Thank you to Renae Holland for her support and her editing.

Thank you to Mike Grigsby for his creative design and input, including the many revisions on the cover design.

Thank you to Stephan Schiffman for writing the Foreword and being supportive of this endeavor.

Thank you to the many leaders who have taught me, inspired me, coached me, poured into me, and lead me to this point in life. I am truly excited about what will come next.

FOREWORD
By Stephan Schiffman
Author of more than 50 books on sales and success

When was the last time you listened to your heart as a leader? I mean, when have you really listened to it? When was the last time that you were able to pick up the rhythm of your body playing out it's life song?

For the longest time, I have wondered why so many people, who have the same heart, and even the same body structure never heard the same beat. Oh, there is no question that some hearts are faster than others are, and there are people whose heart is in the "wrong place". We all do have a beat that we carry with us.

Suppose we were able to get on that beat, and use it to our own advantage as leaders. Wouldn't that be wonderful? We would know where we were going and how we were going to get there. We would have grown to a point of success because we were in rhythm.

The unfortunate fact is that most people never listen hard enough to discern the right rhythm for their lives. The answers are there in front of them. They simply don't get in tune with what needs to happen next in their lives.

I have been working with people for the past 35 years, and I have found that most potential is lost in going from here to there without any meaningful communication. It is as if it does not matter what we do, so long as we get there. Few people ever define where "there" is. Most of us do not know how to use the word "success" and are not sure what it means...many refer to money or something similar.

My guess is that you use GPS when you drive. There is a basic problem with GPS is that it keeps you focused on the immediate, or short-term, directions (turn left, turn right, go 33 miles). You may not actually know where you are unless you see a road sign that informs you. While this is very helpful for getting from point A to point B in the car, it is a poor substitute for directions in life. We need a real picture of who and where we are in order to know where we are going.

We seem to be obsessed with quick elements of doing rather than thinking for ourselves. Very few people think anymore. Instead, they have Google to do that! Try it sometime, just sit down and think though a problem, and see what happens.

Be careful, someone might approach you and ask if you are ok. You are thinking after all. Then they might tell you that you are depressed. You will respond to them indicating that you are thinking. You may find yourself in a much deeper conversation than you intended. After all, so few people know how to think for themselves anymore. It can be quite inspiring for them!

Life is a series of steps that allow you to proceed in the direction that you want to go. First, however, you need to determine where it is that you want to end up, your purpose, and then begin the trip.

Too often, we will "see what happens" rather than "make it happen."

A number of years ago I wrote a book "Make It Happen Before

Lunch" which was based on the famous literary agent Swifty Lazar. His philosophy was to create an action step for one's self that will produce great results. He also knew that the discipline was important, and therefore, each day he stared a project that would offer results in the future; not necessarily immediately.

Maybe that is the way we should all work, thinking out how we are going to create the world as we want it to be, and not someone else's vision of the world. It is in mastering ourselves that we prepare for the future that is right for us.

Defining your purpose and being willing to work towards that end leads you into vision, that escapable "thing" that we talk about but often don't know what it really means. After all, it is more than just seeing possibilities. It setting a goal, evaluating our current skills/location, and fulfilling that dream through learning and action.

If you are reading this book, you are fortunate. Your desire to grow as a leader means that you have the will to be successful....there is that word again. You are a person who is made up of principles that allow you to conquer your fears and move forward. There are so many who do not have that luxury because they have never mastered the skills necessary to get their life and their leadership skills in rhythm. You are lucky because you have chosen to be!

What will you do with that luck? Will you throw it away, or will you take the steps needed to brave the future?

The future, the future, the future, what is that? I do not know nor can I possibly answer what your future is for you. Nevertheless, I know that it is your future and not mine. Our beats are different and yet we are thrust in the same direction. We are thrust toward the betterment of ourselves and the world. We are able to accomplish what we want if we are only given the direction.

Winston Church summed up life in some very simple words. He said, “Never, never, never give up”. The same is true you for now and into your future.

I Wish You All The Best In Your Leadership Success!

Stephan Schiffman

1 THE RHYTHM OF GROWTH

MASTERING THE RHYTHM OF LEADERSHIP SUCCESS

There is a rhythm in this world. This rhythm that I am talking about is rooted in the patterns of thought that exist in your mind. It is a rhythm that defines where we are, who we are, and how far we are able to go in life. There isn't a single person that does not fall prey to hypnotic rhythm. There isn't a single person that makes it through life without being persuaded by the rhythm. The rhythm is neither good, nor bad. It is simply a rhythm. What we do with the rhythm will determine whether it benefits us or holds us back. How we use this rhythm with others determines whether our intent is good or bad. You have an infinite power to be successful, to influence others, and to create good or evil in this world. The question is… what will you do with it?

Have you ever had the experience of leaving your office and driving to your house and then not remembering any part of the trip between the two places? Have you ever performed a task and literally not had to think consciously about the task? If so, you have experienced hypnosis in one of its most basic forms. You have been hypnotized by your conditioning. Most people have had this same experience. They have performed a routine task, one that they had done countless times before, but not consciously thought about what they were doing. Athletes have had this same experience on the field, the court, trail, or in the water. This is often referred to by coaches and athletes as muscle memory. It is when the activity becomes a natural extension of themselves. When a great golfer steps on to the tee-box, they go through a specific ritual that unlocks the appropriate rhythms of success and puts the right motions into action. They place their tee in the ground with their left hand. They brush the grass around the tee to ensure that there is nothing that will interfere with their perfect swing. They place their golf ball, letters to the front, on the tee with the same hand in which they planted the tee. They stand up, left foot pointing on the ground to the final destination of the ball. They step two steps backwards away from the ball and then grasp their club with both hands in a perfect grip, pointing down the fairway to where they will be delivering the ball. They step to the ball, then back one step for their practice swing, ensuring that the rhythm is perfectly in place. They then step into the ideal spot for the execution of the swing. Their brain waves have been consistently changing to that of both hyper-relaxation and hyper-awareness. They are acutely aware of the ball, the fairway, and their connection to the game. They pull the club back into place and then allow the rhythm to propel it forward with every part of their body inline exactly as it should be to execute a perfect swing, yet not thinking of the swing itself. The club and the ball connect with one another and the perfect ping is heard by the golfer. The ball launches on its journey and lands on the green within 3 feet of the hole. We experience beauty and grace and fulfillment when we are in alignment with the rhythm. The golfer holds the club at the end of the swing as he smiles and is grateful for the rhythm.

This is simply one example of when we operate in a hypnotic state and propel ourselves toward success. It happens every day. You use this powerful persuasion technique when you convince your friend to go to a game with you, when you ask a person on a date, and yes… when you lead your people at work. You must master this skill in order to become truly effective as a leader. There are people that have this skill as a part of what was developed in them during their formative years. There are those who are born with personal magnetism. And, there are those that must learn it as adults. Make no mistake though, it can be learned. It can be mastered. The key question that you must answer for yourself is whether or not you are willing to spend the time and focus to develop this skill.

Two critical components of your success as you get started are:

1. You must understand the stages of learning that you will go through to master your communication rhythm.

2. You must develop your purpose and your intent. All the world conspires to help the person who has an absolute purpose.

The four stages of advancement to achieve the right rhythm are:

1. Unconsciously Unskilled: During this stage, you are unaware of any lack of skill because you have not focused on this area. This is the state that the majority of people walking the earth fall into. They don't know that there is more out there, or that they are missing anything in their life. They struggle with life and assume that it is life that chooses who wins and who loses in communication. They don't usually think that they have any choice. They are unaccountable to themselves and operate with a victim's mentality. In order to move out of this stage, one must first be willing to accept that there are things that they don't know and that they need to know in order to take control of life. They must say that they are in the position that they are in because of the choices that they have made. They must accept responsibility for their choices, their lack of success, their situation in life. They must drop blame and accept choice. As soon as they stop blaming the world, their circumstances or other people for where they are, they will become aware of their lack of skill. Their eyes will be opened to the truth of their situation and they will quickly move into the second stage. It is the truth of awareness that sets them free from the bondage of ignorance. However, one must want to be free from ignorance. Not everyone wants that freedom because becoming free means that there are three more stages that lay in front of you. It is often easier to just pretend that nothing is their fault. Are you pretending

that you don't know what you are missing? Are you pretending that there is nothing that you can do to make your communication, your leadership, and your life better? Or, are you ready for the truth and the journey? If you are ready, stage 2 is next.

2. Consciously Unskilled: When someone is consciously unskilled at something, they have accepted responsibility for the fact that they have not learned the skill. They know that it will require work. During this stage, they must explore the collection of their experiences that has led them to where they are at this exact moment. They must look at their evolution and identify points in their history where they could have made different choices. This exercise is extremely important because it will predict what they will do with future opportunities. If we do not explore our past, how can we truly connect with our future? How can we know that the series of present moment choices that we make going forward will be right? During this stage, you are learning where you are and identifying any and all points that you are missing in order to move yourself forward. A complete awareness of what rhythm exists in a person's life is necessary. Without a thorough and critical evaluation of the skills that are present and those that are missing, we can easily slip back into stage one. That will never move you to your fullest potential. You must continuously move forward. By studying what works and what doesn't work, you begin to classify things into their proper categories. You take actions on the things that you believe are your choices. You must create a map of your strengths and what components are missing and you must be brutally honest. This full awareness propels you into learning and growth. The best athletes have coaches. They have someone who

will observe them and who is a master at evaluating others. The coach rarely possesses the same athleticism as the athlete. That isn't the point though. The coach is a master of evaluation and development. The athlete is a master of their sport. All of the greats will have someone who observes them, critiques them, develops them, and pushes them to move forward. Once you have your list of areas that you are not as strong as you would like to be, or need to be to get the right results, then and only then, can you move to stage 3.

3. Consciously Skilled: This stage is what is achieved after you have received sufficient training and development on a skill. How much is enough? Only you can know that. Only you will know when you have achieved the point where your game is at the level that you desire. Remember what you learned about stage 2 though. You must be completely honest with yourself in order to move things forward. When you begin to accept mediocrity or blame anything in the world, then you are regressing. That will never get you to the point of a successful rhythm. During this stage, you must have someone who coaches you, helps you, watches you, corrects you, and invests in you. You must invest in yourself. You have to think through the things that you are doing in order to do them correctly. As long as you are focused and using conscious thought to block out the distractions and remain fully engaged in what you are doing, you can perform the tasks correctly. You are aware of your strengths and weaknesses in this stage. You have taken the time to learn what you need to know in order to be successful. You are consistently performing those tasks in the moment. You have learned to live in the moment and block the past and the future. You are now demonstrating your rhythm

successfully, but it does require that you step through it in your mind each time. In the story of the golfer earlier, he did not spend his time thinking about the way in which he held his head, where his eyes were, the exact placement of his grip, or the perfect width of his feet. All of those things are natural extensions of him now. This is a cellular or muscle memory built from correct training. It takes approximately 2,500 correct repetitions of a skill in order to progress to stage 4. These skills are a part of his rhythm of success. In order to move into stage four with your communication, you will generally have a hypnotic progression that you follow. It is a series of things that you do to fully engage that rhythm within your own mind. You can do the same thing with your employees through effective conditioning. In fact, you already have. You just might not realize the direction in which you have conditioned them. When you shut your door, they know that you are upset and it is a good idea to avoid you. When you sigh deeply, they know that the financials are not where they should be. Any number of things that you do can trigger a response in others. Mastering the triggering events will place you in the position of guiding your team where you want them to be. Moving forward into stage 4 is the goal for each of us as hypnotic communicators and evolved leaders.

4. Unconsciously Skilled: When you are in rhythm, you no longer have to think about what you are doing or what others are doing. Your brain reaches a state of hyper-awareness and yet complete calm at the same time. The trained muscle memory of the mind and body are in control. You are in tune with your environment. Your mind is clear and the parts of the world that are irrelevant to the task at hand simply fade into the

background. It's like looking at a picture with a hidden dimension and you only see the deeper image. You display your skill perfectly and everything seems to flow smoothly back and forth between yourself and those with whom you are communicating. This is the same for any skill for which you have achieved mastery. You are no longer thinking with your conscious mind. You are fully in the moment and completely present with the task at hand. Some people will have a mantra to get themselves mentally prepared, while others have a specific routine that they go through in order to achieve this state. Steven Pressfield, in The War of Art (Pressfield, 2012), refers to this stage as "invoking your Meuse."[1] It is a state of awareness that requires no thought, but connects you to the intelligence that exists and connects all people and all things together. When you are in this state, you are at your highest level of influence. You are exactly who you knew you could always be, and yet it seems to be effortless. That is the way that rhythm works. It is the creation of rhythm that is tough. Once you have achieved the rhythm, you coexist with it. You live in hypnotic communication, you do not perform it. In stage 4, you and the skill are one and the same.

The great challenge is to possess the desire to move through these stages effectively. This challenge is impossible to overcome if you have not developed a definite purpose for your life. With definite purpose, the world will conspire for your success. Napoleon Hill, in his book Outwitting The Devil (Hill, 2012), says that only 2% of people have a definite purpose.[2] This will put you amongst the elite of our world and those who wield great influence. Having a purpose for your life and for the work that you will perform will position you to succeed at the highest levels. The following is a simple exercise that will enable you to learn more about where you truly desire to go.

1. Write down 5 values that you believe best describe you. Examples of this would be things like integrity, success, focus, hard work, and creativity.
    a. ______________________
    b. ______________________
    c. ______________________
    d. ______________________
    e. ______________________

2. Write down 5 action words that describe your focus and best describe you.
    a. ______________________
    b. ______________________
    c. ______________________
    d. ______________________
    e. ______________________

3. Write down 5 ways of describing the results that you want to achieve or expect to receive from your efforts.
    a. ______________________
    b. ______________________
    c. ______________________
    d. ______________________
    e. ______________________

Values, actions, and results work together in order to create a definition of who you are at your core. After you have listed five on each of these areas, you will go back through and eliminate one at a time from each area that is the least descriptive or representative of you in the group of words.

You will continue this process one at a time until you are down to the one that you simply cannot imagine ever living without in your life. This process of elimination has proven to be very effective in helping people to create "right focus" in their lives. Once you are done with the elimination process, simply fill in the blanks below.
The value that best defines who I am is
_________________. I am a person of action and am defined by _________________ as my action every day. The result that I will absolutely achieve is
_________________.
Having a definition of your guiding principles and primary focus area sets you apart from the vast majority of people in this world. Never forget what your defining purpose is as a leader in your field. If you are guided by purpose and driven by passion, you will see that heaven and earth will move to provide you with opportunity. You will find that chance is in your favor, that coincidences happen regularly to set you up for success.

In the next chapter, you will learn the art and science of Hypnotic Communication. If you have ever wanted to be a master of persuasion, particularly as a leader, you will have to master the techniques taught in the next chapter. Think for a moment about a person that you know who seems to have business simply fall into their lap. They are sought after by others on a continuous basis. That person is not just lucky. They are definite in their purpose and masterful in their communication. You can master the techniques as well. You must simply begin to take the right steps to move in that direction. Let's move forward together. I can't wait to hear your stories of success after you learn what the masters know.

2 HYPNOTIC COMMUNICATION
GETTING OTHERS TO WANT TO FOLLOW YOU

He walked into the room full of people. The party was in full swing and he purposely waited until now to make his entrance. He knew that the first person there was seen as eager in school or at work, but desperate in a social gathering. He was not desperate. He had not needed to think any desperate thoughts for some time now. As he walked in, he had a certain bounce to his step, just the right quickness to his pace, and an air of confidence that would scare off predators and attract those who desired leadership. He pictured himself in his spirit as being a benevolent jungle cat, walking into the midst of animals who all desired his favor. His was not an arrogance, but a knowing. He knew that he had something great to offer. He knew that he was emitting a confidence that cannot be spoken with words, but only experienced. He held his head high, his shoulders back, a slightly wry grin on his face, and moved his entire body in one fluid motion as he crossed the room. It was almost as if the room moved for him as the world rotated around him. He had what Napolen Hill had referred to as personal magnetism, what others called mojo, but what he knew to be skill.

He had spent a great deal of time developing the skill of hypnotic communication. He knew that he could read people and adapt to their communication style quickly, then smoothly lead them to follow his style. He approached the woman that he had wanted to meet last year at this party, but didn't have the skillset to make the approach successfully before now. His stride was slightly longer than the average person and he approached her fairly quickly. Without having to be told anything, she spotted him as he was still 20 feet away and tried to look away, but somehow she couldn't. She was fascinated by the confidence that seemed to surround him. She was captivated with the perception that nothing seemed to be in his way. She was curious as to where this man was going and who he was. It only took her a second to realize that he was headed toward her. She awkwardly looked to both sides to see if there was someone else that he was focused on. There wasn't. He was locked in on her. In 5 steps, he had crossed the room. On the 4th step since she had spotted him, his smile grew larger, his eyes opened up as if to reveal a beautiful soul, and his hand went up and extended gracefully out to hers. Without thinking, her hand went up to engage in a firm handshake. Just as their hands touched, he turned her hand slightly to rest on top of his, cocked his head subtly to the left and said, "My name is Cody. It is a pleasure to meet you." For a second, she forgot that it was her turn to speak. After she introduced herself back, the two of them stayed connected for the rest of the evening.

This is just a very small example of what the right non-verbal communication can do for you as you engage with people in your professional and personal life. Cody never stopped talking, but said only two sentences during that entire engagement. As leaders, we must master the jungle that we call life. We must own the space that we exist in and control the flow of energy that is around us and between us and others. This was thought to be impossible to learn by many of the early leaders. It was thought that this presence came from a higher spiritual plane and was either bestowed on or withheld from each person. That isn't true. It is developed and can be developed in anyone that is truly willing to look at life differently. You must be willing to evolve your thought about communication and connection in order to fully grasp the power and simplicity of hypnotic communication. Mastering this one section alone will set you apart from 90% of all people. You will be the girl or guy that everyone wants to be connected with the moment they enter the room. The problem that most people have is that they never take the time to learn these skills, even though they are clearly what sets the charismatic leaders apart from the rest of the world.

Let's dive into this subject so that you can begin learning the principles of owning the space around you and creating your own gravitational pull as a leader. Many people find their greatest results in being coached through this process at one of our live events. (Information in the back of the book.) Your objective should be to master the skills that create that leadership draw that others cannot resist. There are the three components that must be mastered in order to move yourself to the top of food chain as a communicator.

Hypnotic communication has the following components inside of it.

You must develop your non-verbal communication skills. This includes your use of tone and pitch, facial expression, and body language.

You must develop your physical presence. You have to own the air around you and command attention from others.

You must master the ability to read others and respond appropriately. Your ability to read their non-verbal signals will provide you with the necessary information to retool your approach when necessary, to adapt as needed, or to redirect if the need arises.

Mastery of each of these skills is not an overnight event. You must develop these skills to the point of them operating in that rhythmic state. This means that you will pass through four stages of development with each of the skills in order to achieve mastery.

Mastering your non-verbal signals that are sent is not a simple decision to get in touch with your emotions. It is a choice to control the emotions that others read on you. If you have ever been told by someone that they can "read you like a book," then you have displayed your non-verbal communication. The problem is, that was not really a compliment. That was a person telling you that you are mostly unaware of what you are portraying. Mastery of self includes being able to portray the right, or desired, emotions on command.

Think back to when you were young and your mother, father, teacher, or guardian told you: Don't talk to me in that tone of voice. The first few times that you were told to change your tone, you were unsure of what they were trying to get across. Your tone, you came to understand, was the way in which your words left your tongue. You were not generally taught in school how to present your right tone, or how to come across as pleasing, aggressive, agitated, or happy. You simply said what you were thinking at the time. Tone can be thought of as the presentation of words in such a way that the meaning of the word is made more clear because of the naturally interpreted sound. The way in which the words roll off of your tongue will paint a picture clearly for the other person to see. If we paint a pleasing picture, then the person we are communicating with will want to marvel in the beauty that is before them. They will "feel" like responding in the right manner to our communication and giving us what we want. If our words paint an ugly or immature picture in the ether, the person will look at the picture and will not be motivated to respond in the right manner. It will turn their stomach and make them want to focus in a different direction. Take a minute to visualize the most engaging speaker or conversationalist that you know. Hear their words in your mind. Try to bring the experience of listening to them or engaging with them fully into your mind. Allow the positive emotions to well up inside of you, just as they did the last time you listened to that person.

The right pitch and tone in your voice makes others want to be around you. If you have ever been frustrated by the fact that others don't listen to you, or that they don't do what you ask, then you have not effectively gotten your message across through non-verbal communication. The first question you should have asked and you should ask now is, what can I do different? The mistake we make is to think that others are supposed to change for us whether they want to or not. The truth is that people only change when they want to change. Picture the last conversation with another person that did not go well. What did their face look like? What did their body look like? Think back to what you said and how you said it. Picture the way that the conversation appeared from the outside. During our Leadership Evo weekends, we teach the specific skills of listening, non-verbal engagement, and give real-time feedback on how to adjust your pitch and tone to be the best. A few techniques that will help you with your practice are as follows…

Learn to vary your voice. This is also known as paralinguistic communication. Merriam Webster (Merriam-Webster Online, 2013) dictionary defines paralanguage as the optional vocal effects (such as tone of voice) that help to create meaning in communication. Mastering your vocal effects will set you apart from others in your field. You will want to ensure that you do not use the same tone of voice throughout your talking. Make the tone go up and down to mirror the up and down thoughts that you are expressing. The same would be true for the pitch of your voice. You want to vary the rhythm by speeding up when the listener should be excited and slowing down for a dramatic point or to drive a point home. When telling stories, even work related stories, you should change the volume of your speech as well. Be aware of the age of your audience on this one as being too soft is annoying for an audience that has more trouble hearing. Finally, the inflection and emphasis on aspects of the words becomes important. Think about some of the greatest speakers and presenters that you have heard. Each of them understood how to keep the audience interested. The audience was interested, because the speaker shared their information in an interesting way. It is not the information that is always interesting. It is, rather, the way in which that information is presented that makes it interesting.

Learn to use gestures appropriately. You will want to exaggerate these when you are giving a public speech. The greatest speakers in the world use dramatic gestures with their hands, head, eyes, and even their entire body. For example, if you would normally gesture openness by lifting your hands to waist high and then putting your palms up, you move your hands out with your elbows still close to your body, then do it larger and more open in a speech. In a speech, you would have the same starting position but you would push your entire arms out and make a much larger outward swing with your hands and arms. Proper exaggeration during a speech will better engage your audience.

Learn to read and adapt to cultural norms. This one can be a little tougher. I would encourage you, if you deal with a lot of varied cultures, to continue studying intercultural communication. A few basics that you need to focus on for the purposes of this section are spacial orientation, eye contact and the hand-shake. In interviewing, most interviewers will make up the majority of their mind about a person within the first 10 seconds of communication with that person. When you are at a party or in a social setting, the same is true. When you learn to approach others with what comes across as confidence, then you have the highest likelihood of being seen as a super-star, great person, intelligent, and all of the other adjectives that describe somebody that we want to be around. Take large strides as you enter a room and when you are wanting to shake someone's hands, make eye contact early. Don't stare at the floor or look sheepish. One step before you get to the person, pull your right elbow back just to the back of your torso/side and raise that hand simultaneously. On the last step, lean your body forward slightly and extend your hand to clasp the hand of the person you wish to engage with. Match the grip of their handshake. Do not try to crush their hand to prove that you are stronger. Match their grip. Look them in the eye as you say hello and say your name. As they say their name, respond back with their first name and "it's a pleasure to meet you." Most people forget this norm of being seen as a great person by the introduction. But, first impressions really are lasting impressions. You will generally hold their hand for approximately 3 seconds as you shake hands. Release their hand and ensure that you have at least a full arm's length of space between you and the other person. Next, picture in your mind the name of the person as a graphic or sign above their head and repeat their name in your mind three times while seeing this mental image. You do not need to close your eyes as you do this. That would make you look weird. When dealing with other cultures, including people from various parts of your own country, be sure to watch a couple of people greet each other and then mirror their behavior patterns. By blending with the cultural norms, you are more readily accepted and are seen as more intelligent. To know this is true, all you have to do is travel to another country and act just like you would at home. Then, watch to see the reactions of the people around you. If you display behavioral patterns that are outside of the norms, you will be treated as if you are less intelligent, or arrogant, or simply incapable of connecting. People from other countries will respond the most positively to you when you are similar to them. Every part of every country has norms or expectations for the behavioral interaction while communicating. Learn through observation and adapt to be the best. After all, most people want to be around people that believe, think, and behave the way that they do.

Learn to use humor and humorous response elicitation. A humorous response elicitation is a way in which you connect with people that helps them to laugh at inconsistencies or quick thought pattern changes. Comedians have used inconsistencies as a way to help stimulate memory and trigger this response. We pay so much for entertainment because we want to be around people who change our perspective. People like people who make them smile. Some people, however, struggle more with this one than others. They often struggle because their non-verbal communication says that they are arrogant and then they try to be funny. Funny and arrogant don't blend well. If you are traditionally seen as overly proud of who you are, you will likely only be funny to yourself. Step 1 in this area is to get over yourself and learn to laugh at and make fun of yourself. The use of directional switching (quick switches in thought pattern) is a great way to get people to smile. Great comedians use this as a part of their routines regularly. In training programs that I teach on time management, I start with the following story… "Have you guys seen those women that are putting on their makeup while they are driving? I saw one this morning on the way to this training. We were coming down the interstate/highway and I looked over and saw this lady putting on mascara. She was adjusting her eye-lid with one hand and putting on mascara with the other. About that time, her car began to drift into my lane. It freaked me out. I dropped my cell phone in my cup of coffee that was between my legs and lost the entire egg out of the sandwich that was in my other hand. Those dang multi-taskers drive me crazy." When you tell that story with some dramatic inflection in your voice, the normal response is a delayed laugh at the fact that I was doing something worse than what I was griping about. Being good at being the butt of the joke is an art and requires that you really are a confident person who does not look down on anyone else. If you look down on people with less education, people feel it in your communication. To be funny, you start by loving and respecting all people. That may sound a little "Miss-America-ish" as an answer, (My biggest goal if I am selected is to achieve world peace.), but it really does make a huge difference. Be a great person and be confident enough to be laughed at. This makes all the difference on humor. If you cannot handle other people laughing at you, you are likely in for a great deal of stress in your life. You will also struggle more with leadership than others.

Your physical presence is the next, and perhaps most important aspect of how you communicate without words, particularly as a leader. Your physical presence is the complete way in which you carry yourself into a room, in a conversation, or giving a speech. You need to come across as a confident leader who wants to lead others to victory. You need to be the best quarterback in the world, the king of the jungle, the silver-back ape, and the great white shark all rolled into one. As a mighty warrior, though, you see everyone around you as desiring your success, because they know it makes them better as well. This internal confidence will come across in the way you walk, talk, smile, and lead others. If you are absolutely confident in who you are and what you have to offer the world, then you walk with a smile on your face, a spring in your step, and a swing to your stride. You own whatever room when you enter. Your walk is slightly quicker than the average person. You keep your shoulders back and your chin up wherever you go. You are confident and happy. Take a minute to picture the most confident and happy person that you know. Get an image in your mind of what they look like. Picture how they walk and talk. See how they interact with others. Once you have that image in your mind, all you really have to do is imitate that person. It is said that imitation is the greatest form of flattery. Make sure to separate the arrogant people from the confident people in the pursuit of the perfect person to imitate. Arrogance is a turn-off. Some people may give the arrogant person what they want temporarily, but that person will always end up losing out. You can identify an arrogant person because their relationships are short-lived or very superficial. They often attract people with no confidence to follow them. The confident person attracts other confident people and brings out the confidence in others.

To practice this, start each day by smiling for a minimum of two minutes straight. Then, recite the following as you look at yourself in the mirror with the perfect posture and facial expression:

Today, I own my day. People love being around me, because I bring out the best in them and display the best in myself. I am a winner and make other people winners by being around them. I will carry myself like the winner that I am! I will inspire others to smile, laugh, and succeed today.

This simple affirmation, when done every morning, will set your day onto the right path. Never forget that the way in which you carry yourself is your choice. You are not a product of your circumstances. In fact, you control your emotions by controlling your physiology. The more confident you see yourself, the easier it will be for you to carry yourself that way. The more you practice carrying yourself confidently, the more likely you will be to feel confident and own the space that you exist in. So, see yourself as having a lot to offer and you will begin to have a lot to offer. For great practice on this, consider attending one of our Leadership Evo weekends. The back of this book will have information on how you can do that.

Reading others is one of the critical components of your emotional intelligence. Your ability to read the facial expressions, tone of voice, and body language of others will set you apart from the rest of the crowd. It will also make you truly hypnotic. One of the main reasons that others are drawn to you, and will want to find ways to assist you in your success, is your ability to read and understand their needs. Reading others and learning to be a great listener comes with practice and an understanding of what a great listener is like. As you are listening to others, you must first pay attention to them with your eyes. This means that you will need to avoid distractions and stay focused just on that person. Put away your phone. Turn off your email. Stop reading that book. Focus on them. If you are not fully focused on that person, giving them your undivided attention, then they will not open up to you and will not see you as an empathetic person. The second component is to ask questions that get them talking more and explaining their position. The problem that most people have with persuasion is that they are focused only on their point of view and purpose. When you listen to the other person, they will tell you what you need to know in order to persuade them. For example, in selling, you would ask open ended questions of the person about their processes, their desires, their hopes, and what they wish they had that they don't currently have. Once they explain all of this, you will know where they are, where they want to be, and what they think is missing. As long as you offer the solution to fill the gap of what is missing, you will be seen as a hero, not a product pusher. The third aspect of this process is to paraphrase the underlying message and emotion that you have gotten from the other person. This means that you will need to listen for emotion in their sentences and then interpret that into your own words. You never want to simply repeat the other person. You want to interpret what they are saying and check for understanding. Your objective in reading the other person is to get a full understanding of where they are coming from and where they want to go. When you communicate, you are projecting your message through your facial expressions, body language, paralanguage (dress and appearance) and tone of voice. Each person that communicates with you is doing the same thing. Most communicators just don't realize what they are doing. If you practice listening and reading others, you will position yourself as a truly hypnotic communicator.

The skills in this chapter, more so than the others, can really best be developed in person at one of our conferences. I am sure you will be practicing these skills and will want to be the best communicator possible. I am also sure, based on past experiences, that you will be thinking of these skills as you interact with others over the next several months. As you focus on becoming a master communicator, seek out ways to practice and hone your hypnotic communication skills. Links to helpful videos and resources can be found at www.LeadershipEvo.com. Hypnotic communicators are inspiring leaders!

3 WORKPLACE EVANGELISTS
HOW BUILDING THE TEAM CHANGES EVERYTHING

Within any workplace, the objective should be and often is to create a fully functional team of people who believe so deeply in the company that they can't keep their mouths shut. An evangelist is someone who believes that they possess the truth and passionately shares what they believe with others. They are the people who cannot be stopped, because they know with absolute certainty that where they are is woven into the fabric of their purpose. That level of conviction is not easily attained, but is absolutely sought after. An evangelist goes beyond someone who has a strong liking for, or even a belief in a company, product, or purpose. An evangelist has faith; faith that cannot be reasoned with. It is not shaken by temporary setback. It is not easily defeated, derailed, or detained. It fires employees up and focuses them on what is important so that they can avoid those things that are not. There are distinctive stages and key skills that must be mastered in order to turn an organization into one filled with the unshakable, fired up and focused evangelists.

Let's take a look at what a company full of evangelists looks like versus a company of employees.

The story of Emily is one that many of us long to experience, but seldom have the chance to live. I will let her tell it from her own perspective.

As I write this, it is 6 a.m. on Monday morning and I can't wait to get to work. My team put in time over the weekend on our latest product. We are still several months away from launch, but we know that it has the power to reshape communication in the workplace and make team collaboration so much more functional. Anyway, it isn't the product that you asked me about. You asked me about what drives me at my job. Actually, I have trouble thinking of it as a job. It is really a part of who I am. I think of it as an extension of myself. When I went to work for this company 2 years ago, I was looking for a job. I had been working for another software company as a team lead, and I was burned out. My boss yelled at me a lot, because he yelled at everybody a lot. We had good products, but nothing to write home about. We were alright though, because we made money and we knew that we had market share with stable jobs. That pretty well fits the description that my parents had given me of what to strive for in life. However, I didn't just want security. I wanted to be a part of something that actually could make a difference. I wanted to be connected with a mission and with passionate people who saw what they were doing for a living as a part of the grand design for moving this world forward. I didn't want mediocrity. I wanted something that changed the world and, therefore, changed me. When I first went to work here, my new boss told me that this job would likely be more difficult and a much larger challenge than anything that I had experienced before. She told me that she would push me harder and demand more of me than my other supervisors. She also told me that she would celebrate more with me when I succeeded. She taught me that my success was my choice. The thing that really sticks out though from that speech was that they did not allow people to work here who weren't on fire about the product and the opportunity. That really struck me, because what I had seen in my previous work was that I was rewarded the same as everyone else, regardless of the amount of work that I did or the results that I produced. We spent time together for the first couple of weeks while she showed me the business and taught me what she expected of me. During that time, she made it clear that it was her expectation that I deal with conflict in the workplace as it happened. She also taught me how to do that. After that lesson, came the lesson on intended outcomes. She said that most companies get stuck in a rut of "good enough" and never push themselves to be the best. She said that she only wanted people who wanted to change the world in our area on her team. She said that she would not have any hard feelings if I didn't want to work that hard or make that big of a difference, but I needed to decide right then what I was going to do with the rest of my life. Was I going to be a game changer or simply play the game? I was inspired and that isn't something that I remember ever being before at work. I wanted to change the game. I wanted to climb a mountain, wrestle a bear, leap over tall buildings and run to the rooftop to tell people how awesome this was going to be for the world. I remember that day starting down the path to being an evangelist for this company. I began telling people about our products and about our opportunities regularly. It takes physical restraint even now to simply talk about that experience and not to talk about our new team collaboration software. I hope this helps. I have faith in my boss, faith in my team, and faith in the future of this company!

Sincerely,

Emily

Emily is on fire because she and the team that she is on evolved through four stages. These are stages that a person must be lead through. You cannot force or push your people to go through the stages. You can only lead them. Your leadership is defined solely by your positive influence with others and is measured by your ability to lead people forward. The four stages that you will learn are as follows…

1. Team Creation – Standardizing success and connecting talent
2. Team Communication – Creating good conflict and cooperation
3. Team Acceleration – Decision models and strengths focus
4. Team Evangelism – Faith, balance, and extension of self

Dr. Bruce Tuckman came up with the four stages of team development in 1965 at Ohio State University (Tuckman, 1965). He defined them as forming, storming, norming, and performing. In the early 1970's, he added the 5th stage, known as adjourning. Tuckman's research has been the basis for discussion for many of the theories on how to develop your teams as well as to understand calculating what level your team was at in the process. Using some of that same thought process, you will be able to see how you can take your team to the highest level of focus and performance.

To create the right team, there are four basic things you must have. You must have: the right standards, the right people, the right development of those people, and the right relational connectivity. You have to be very careful as to how you approach this section because it is the foundation for what comes next and what you will end up with at the end. I would argue that very few organizations have any standards for the types of people that they are looking for. Our world has gotten to the point of watering down everything in an attempt to not hurt people's feelings. We have job descriptions, but we don't have standards. We don't keep score in Little League and then put those same kids to work where they are unsure of why we would judge their work at all. It is the measurement that makes the person. It is the scrutiny that determines what is revealed. If you want to have a team of evangelists, you have to define what superstars look like. As a leader, your job is to build the right team. If you don't have the right team, it is very likely that it started at this point with "giving people a break" or lowering your standards for who got on your team. STOP! Let's take a look at what you really want on your team. In putting together you team, you want to evaluate fit and then skill. It has been a common business mis-practice to seek out skill and then try to make them fit. In an interview by the BBC (Jobs, 1996), 11 years after John Sculley outmaneuvered Jobs in a Boardroom dispute over strategy, Jobs laments that he recruited the wrong guy. Steve Jobs learned a valuable lesson… wrong fit means wrong person. John's focus was on self-success and not on changing the world through Apple. Jobs was demoted in his own company, eventually resulting in his resignation, and Apple took a sharp nose-dive. One person does make all the difference in the world. When Apple bought NeXT and Jobs came back to Apple, we were given the Macintosh, the iPod, the iPhone, the iMac and more. Jobs learned the lesson of setting the values standards very high with that misstep and it was a lesson that he never forgot. Take a few minutes and fill in the blanks on what values are most important in defining your team.

Team Values:

1. ______________________________

2. ______________________________

3. ______________________________

These should be the three values that are most important to your team. They should be taught to the people that join your team and drilled in regularly at meetings. They should be easy to understand and most importantly, they MUST be lived. If your members fully understand and embrace the values of your team, they are very likely to push towards the next level of team evolution. Having the three driving values of the team, you must never forget that a team is only a team when they are together. This doesn't mean that they have to be physically in each other's presence. It means that they must be together in spirit. They must feel that they are connected with one another and define themselves in that way. This takes time, communication and the effective building of relationships. When a new member enters your team, you have to get the team together and promote the person to the rest of the team. You want to avoid the "eat their young" mentality that exists in so many workplaces today. You want to build the confidence and connectivity of the members to the point that they define themselves as a team. If they see themselves as a group or a collection of individual talent, you will not be able to move them forward towards that evangelical minded team that cannot help but succeed at every turn. They must define themselves as a team and others must define them that way as well.

Team Evolution – Phase 2: Communication

The second phase of growth and change for the team is that of effective communication. You learned, in depth, how to communicate with your teams in the chapter on Hypnotic Communication, but there are a few basic principles that must be mastered here in order to help the team evolve into its highest potential. By investing in the relational skills of your team early on, skills like conflict resolution and interpersonal communication, this phase of growth will go much smoother. If you avoid the tough challenges of team life, mostly centered around communication and relationship, then this can be a bit tricky to get through. In my experience over the last 15 years of working with companies of all sizes, the vast majority of them get to the beginning of this phase and simply refuse to invest in their people in order to move forward.

The characteristics of a great team that must be mastered in this phase are that of Confrontation, Conflict Resolution, and Advanced Interpersonal Relationships. Tuckman, in his 1965 paper on Developmental Sequence in Small Groups (Tuckman B. W., 1965), referred to this section as the storming stage, and for good reason. During this phase of development, it is critical that you initiate confronting others in the group. It is critical that you master the resolution of conflict, and perhaps more important, that you learn to tie it all together with great communication.

Confronting people is not as difficult as most people make it out to be. It is true that certain personality types have less trouble with confronting than others do, but it can be done by anyone. It is the anticipation of the conflict that is actually worse than the conflict itself. One of the base level fears that we experience is the fear of criticism. Another is the fear of loss of love. This accounts for 33% of the key fears that hold us back in life, and they are both present when we are thinking about confronting another person. In my experience, the facing of the fear is the only act that can overcome the fear. Therefore, in order to overcome your fear of conflict, you have to identify your fears and then take action in the face of them. When you confront another person, you want to be prepared for the conversation and you want to know what to avoid. The following 4 keys are what you must keep in mind as you confront someone...

1. Never focus on the person being confronted. When you talk about them as a person, you escalate the conflict instead of resolving it. We naturally put our defenses up when we feel that someone is coming after us as a person. Always focus on the behavior that is the problem. Describe the behavior that is the problem in nonjudgmental terms. (This means that if a person is late to work by 15 minutes, you don't make references such as when you are lazy, or when you disrespect the team.) Those are judgments or interpretations of the behavior and will stop the positive flow of communication. Instead, simply say, you were 15 minutes late to work.
2. Speak for yourself. An employee once went into his boss to say that everyone was mad at them. The boss replied, "That is impossible. I haven't met them all yet."

The validity of your argument is dependent on you speaking for yourself. People cannot argue with the reality of how you feel or what you are interpreting. That doesn't mean that your interpretation is correct every time. It simply means that your interpretation is yours. You don't know the mind of another person. You only know yours, so only speak for you.

3. Describe the measurable effect of the other person's behavior. When you want to make a valid point about the behavior of another person, you have to be able to justify why it is a problem. This means that you need to be able to describe what their behavior is costing, has cost, or could cost you. It must be measurable. If you can't describe what something is costing you, then it is not a conflict of needs. It is a conflict of values. That means that you simply don't like what they are doing. An example would be that Bob doesn't like classical music. Jane does and she plays it quietly at her desk. Bob can't hear the music at Jane's desk, unless he gets up from his desk and walks by her desk. It doesn't disturb his work. He just doesn't like it; it conflicts with his values. If Jane was playing her music at the highest volume, and Bob could not hear the customer on the phone in order to take care of them, the conflict would change to one of needs, because it is now measurable.
4. Make it stick with emotion. The final component of the confrontation is that of describing the emotional response you have had to the event. Anger is the tip of the iceberg, and is generally preceded by some other emotion. Think through to what the base level emotion is that you are feeling before you simply say that something makes you angry. Were you embarrassed first? If so, use embarrassed instead of angry. The more genuine your emotion, the more real it will come across

to the person you are confronting. Putting these components together will position you to be able to get your message across clearly. After you confront though, you do have to listen. You will learn the skill of listening as a part of the chapter on Hypnotic Communication. Pay close attention to the process, because it will be invaluable in diffusing tension and moving people forward.

Acceleration is about taking the team that now knows how to disagree in a positive manner and positioning them for accelerated growth. It is about making great decisions. This process is about using the best parts of each person in order to accelerate the already positive growth the team is experiencing as they come out of the second phase. There are two areas that must be mastered during this phase in order to truly experience the accelerated success you desire with your team. Those two areas are:

1. Focusing on the strengths of each team member
2. Making good decisions

It sounds very natural to think that you would want to focus on the strengths of a person, rather than their weaknesses, but it happens so seldom that it sometimes seems impossible. Our education system conditioned us to focus on the things that we were not good at until we finally became good at those things. If you didn't do well in math, then you took math, were tutored in math, studied math, and practiced math until you mastered the skill of math. The students who received the greatest amount of attention in math class were the ones that did the worst at math. The students that received the least attention were the ones that did best at math. After all, they already knew the basics and educators needed to focus on those with the least. This resulted in and still results in teaching to the lowest common denominator. Without getting political, I want to draw a separation from education and the world of success at work. At work, we should never lead to the lowest common denominator. We should always lead to the highest standard. If someone is not good at something, make every effort to find something that they are good at on your team. If they are not good at anything on your team, or if they choose to not put in the right effort on your team, then give them the opportunity to excel somewhere else. My observation about performance is that people operate on a standard distribution of performance. Roughly, 20% of people have no desire to perform and probably never will, at anything. 20% of people are top performers and will seek out an environment where that is supported, rewarded and recognized. They know what they are good at and spend time every day doing the things that make them shine. The other 60% of people are watching to see where the attention goes. They will begin to perform like those who get the greatest amount of attention. The choice that you are making with these folks is whether you want them to be more like the non-performers or the top-performers. If you want top performance, focus on that. This means that you absolutely have to focus on the strengths of each person on your team and find ways to get people to operate in their strength zones. If you did your part as a leader and built a diverse team, then you should have diverse strengths that compliment each other. The strengths of the collective team should fill all the gaps. This also means that each person must fully recognize their weaknesses and ask for help from someone strong in that area whenever necessary. If we try to operate in our own weaknesses because we are too arrogant to ask for help, then failure will be our cruel teacher. If we try to operate in our strengths and allow others to help in our weaknesses because those are their strengths, the success we have will be our uplifting teacher. Which will you choose? Which have you chosen?

The second aspect of accelerating the team is to have a solid decision making and problem solving model that you follow. Processes and systems will help to protect the team against itself. In other words, human nature is often what gets in the way of success. According to T. Harv Eker in his book Secrets of The Millionaire Mind (Ecker, 2005), the mind's job is to be right, even if that means that you have to lose in order to achieve that. The trick is to be willing to be wrong so that the team can be right. Making good decisions as a team begins with creating a one-goal focus for the team. If we are all going to the same destination, then it is much easier to be objective in the decisions that are made to get there. A trick that will help to keep the team on track as they make decisions is to rotate members as the "devil's advocate" in the process. In making the decisions that affect your team, use the following questions…

1. Will this direction support the stated values of the team? If no, don't move forward. If yes, answer the next question.
2. Will this direction support the stated goals of the team? If no, don't move forward. If yes, answer the next question.
3. Will this direction be what is best for our employees? If no, don't move forward. If yes, answer the next question.
4. Will this direction be what is best for the people we serve? If no, don't move forward. If yes, answer the next question.

5. Will this direction be best for society? If no, don't move forward. If yes, answer the next question.
6. Who is responsible for which aspects of making this happen?
7. What is the timeline for making it happen?
8. How will we measure our success?

If you will focus on making good decisions that are not controlled by a single person, usually the loudest and most intimidating, then favor will follow you.

If you will focus on utilizing the strengths of each of your team members whenever you get the chance, then favor will follow you. You will move quickly from a team that is good, to one that is incredible. This will move your team into the fourth stage where you develop the final attributes of an evangelical team.

Evangelism as a team is about having true faith in the leadership as well as in the company. On a ropes course (adventure learning course), you are tasked with testing your faith in your team. The first time that I jumped off of the challenge pole, I was asked to share wisdom before the jump. If you are unfamiliar with a challenge pole, it is a telephone pole that is 30 feet in the air. You climb to the top and stand on the top of the pole, harnessed in to a belay system, and then jump. Your team on the ground is supposed to control your descent to the ground and keep you safe. My wisdom on that first jump was that trust is believing that your team will catch you, but faith was jumping without fear. It is one thing to think that your team wants the best for you. It is something else entirely to let go of the fear of failure and fall into the arms of your team. It is the definite purpose that can be seen in the faces, felt in the hearts, and displayed in the minds of the team that propels them into faithful evangelists. The term evangelist denotes a person who knows the truth and chooses to share it. When you absolutely know that something is true, you can't help but share it. You have to share it! In order to develop faith in the teams that you lead, you have to utilize auto-suggestion (reinforce repetition of a stated direction) to solidify the definite purpose of the team in their minds. You should start your meetings by stating the intended purpose of the organization or department. You should state the values that drive the organization. Finally, you should state that you are fulfilling a purpose that is bigger than any individual, but is ideal for this team. You are building the thought patterns of your team, which will then build the beliefs, actions and results of your team. Make no mistake, the best companies in the world are led by leaders who have evolved past commonality. They are the leaders who understand how to bring out the absolute belief in a team and keep the team fired up and focused on the dream.

This next part can be a little tricky. The individual members of the team must maintain balance in their lives while believing absolutely in the direction of the team. Balance is defined differently for different people. Each person knows when they are out of balance, but very few people know how to define it without the experience. Each person needs to have adequate time with their family and friends. They need to have a separation from work that allows them to play the various roles in their lives. They need to have an outlet for stress. Finally, they need to have a spiritual connection. Each of these areas is critically important to the financial and workplace success that the person achieves. As a leader, you will need to watch your team and notice when their patterns stray too much. You will need to push them to stay in balance. They need to work enough to be successful and to support the success of their teammates. This is one of the components of balance. They also need to be happy and successful in their work. Being happy is a good indicator of actual balance. Your mind often tells you that it needs a new approach by pushing you away from something or towards something. Pay attention to the signs. Do not, however, succumb to the whims of today's society that sells the elixir of misery at every turn. Don't allow the world to tell you that you should be and deserve to be unhappy. Advertisers need you to believe that you are unhappy so you will ask your doctor about that new drug, buy that item that is supposed make you become magically surrounded by happy people in swimsuits, and on and on. Happiness is a choice to be successful in all areas of your life. You may have to get out of your own way to do that, but it is still a choice. Help your team make the choice to be happy. Invest in them as people and in their success. You must be evangelical about their success BEFORE they will be evangelical about you and the company.

You know that you are a top performer. Your objective is to get others to demonstrate the same behaviors and achieve the same success. Essentially, you are trying to create an extension of yourself. The assumption is being made that if you have gotten your team to this level, then you must be at that level or above. You can only develop from your knowledge and experience. The more you learn about leading and the more you grow personally, the greater the capacity you will have to help your team succeed. The day that you believe that you know everything that you need to know is the day that your team begins to go backwards. They don't even stagnate, they regress.

"Education is the kindling of a flame, not the filling of a vessel." --Socrates (Socrates)

To extend who you are, invest in who they can be. Invest in the possibility of a great person. Expect the behaviors of a top performer. Be very disappointed if you don't get those behaviors. Be overwhelmed with happiness when you do. You only achieve what you invest in. Steve Jobs invested 60 million dollars in Pixar, which he bought for 10 million dollars (All About Steve Jobs Website), before they made Toy Story and changed the face of animated movies. He believed in the team that he had assembled and demonstrated that by pushing them harder than they had ever been pushed. He made them into more than they could have been on their own. He accomplished his vision, his extension of self, through the team. You can do the same, but you must consistently and continuously invest in them!

If you follow the four phases as a pathway to evangelical success with your team, you will see amazing results in the motivation and inspiration of the team members. In order to make this lasting and change the world, one team member at a time, you will need the right skills for delivering your message. While it is true that you don't have to be charismatic to be a great leader, it is the charisma that charms people into desperately wanting to follow your lead. In the last chapter, you learned the art of hypnotic communication. This art, once thought of as impossible, can be mastered through the steps that you read. In the next chapter, you will learn about the four evolutionary styles of leadership. As you read the chapter, stopped periodically and get a picture in your mind of people who fit each of the four descriptions. By thinking about the people that you have experiences with, you will be able to see the importance of moving your own style forward. Your leadership style will ultimately determine the effectiveness of your team being able to move forward. To create the team of evangelists that will continuously promote your business, you have to first develop you.

4 LEADERSHIP EVO STYLES
WHY WE STILL HAVE MONKEYS

This chapter is going to be a fun read and will hopefully help you understand how we have evolved, or in some cases not evolved, our styles of leadership in the workplace. The idea for this book came originally from the Geico® commercial with the cave men. The marketing strategy behind "so easy a cave man could do it" really made me start thinking about the idea of evolving our leadership styles. We have, in fact, evolved our styles and our behaviors over the years. Frederick Taylor, for example, introduced us the concept of scientific management (Wikipedia). He said that leading people is a mechanistic function that involves simple rewards and punishment. If you dangle rewards (carrots) in front of people, they will want to behave as you asked in order to get those carrots into their pockets. He said that people will avoid punishment (sticks) because they are afraid of them. His premise comes from the psychological fact that we are ultimately only motivated by pain or pleasure. The problem is understanding what pain is and what pleasure is and what the lasting effects of those really are, both good and bad. In this chapter, I will present you with my interpretations of where we have been and where we are headed as a leadership community. In order to do that, I need to make sure you have a little background on me and my upbringing. I believe it is most relevant for this chapter.

I grew up the son of a Methodist preacher. My parents are very strong Christians and believe whole-heartedly in Creationism. Even though I am not advocating for the teaching of Darwin's Theory of Natural Selection instead of Creationism in the schools, I would imagine the title of this book with the word EVO, implying evolution, will still give them some heartburn. I feel that I have always had a scientific mind. I like to explore concepts and believe that being open-minded is very important. As a young man, I remember the first time that I was exposed to Darwin's theory. At first, I dismissed it crying, "Heresy, heresy!" Okay, so I really just though, "well that's stupid." Then, I started to explore it further, remembering that we are not supposed to judge. Darwin's theory basically said that in order to become stronger, we must learn to adapt. He said that adaptation was natural, and required, for the survival of a species. I remember my teacher explaining these things to us and then I remember thinking… "But why do we still have monkeys?" I was not one to hold my tongue or restrain from communicative interaction. That being said, I love exploring ideas, despite my initial reaction to some, and I love debate. That means that I was annoying to several of my teachers, funny to others, and thought provoking to the rest. The central question that I needed answered in order to believe that evolution, as a theory, might have any merit was the one I asked. Understanding why some animals get left behind is a critical answer that must be addressed in order to understand why some leaders still focus on leading in a way that doesn't work.

Answer this question, if you can. Why do we still have leaders that yell and curse at their employees? That is a much trickier question than some might think. We still have personality clashes to deal with, egos that pull leaders in the wrong direction, and simple frustration. For this chapter, I am going to give you my four stages of leadership evolution. Keep in mind that each leader has the option of evolving into the best leader possible. In order to evolve though, leaders must do three things.

1. Leaders must recognize their weaknesses and want to overcome them.
2. Leaders must seek out a more evolved leader and learn from them – still dropping the ego.
3. Leaders must face challenges that make them stronger.

At each of the leadership stages, I will lay out what the weaknesses and strengths of the level are. I will also talk about what they should be seeking out in order to grow and evolve. The four stages of leadership evolution are:

1. The Missing Link
2. The Cave Man
3. The Executive
4. Super Leader

The Missing Link

The Missing Link is significantly more common than most of us would like to admit. They are running around the workplace, yelling at their teams, getting mad when the team doesn't know what they are supposed to do, and generally creating messes. This leader doesn't spend time with the team, building relationships, nor do they actually communicate their expectations. They withhold information that would be very beneficial, sometimes even necessary, to their people's success so that they can hold control and power over others. They are very good at manipulation, coercion, and tactics involving forcing other people to do what they want them to do. While many people will think that this person sounds awful, it doesn't necessarily mean that they don't accomplish a lot through others. Fear is their great weapon. They understand that the largest dinosaur with the biggest teeth is the one that gets the prize. They spend their lives looking for how others can help them and what they can get from others. They don't often realize what they are taking or that people don't like them. You can tell a Missing Link by the following five characteristics.

1. They are very poor listeners. The Missing Link is continuously scanning their environment for danger and opportunity. They tend to not focus on what is right in front of them because that is already taken care of. They are not really interested in what the person in front of them has to say anyway. They are not interested because it is the next BIG deal that matters most. As poor listeners, they rely on their ability to push and talk and annoy instead of their ability to influence and persuade. Poor listeners do not look at or focus on the person that they are with. They don't

accurately read the non-verbal communication of others. They don't ask questions of others to clarify points that they might have missed. They fill in the gaps with what they think should be there instead of what the other person meant to be there in the message. And finally, they do not accurately read the emotions of others in a conversation. They often assume that people really like them because they like themselves so much. I am sure at this point that you are thinking of someone that you have worked with or are currently working with. If you are a Missing Link, you would not have made it this far in the book.

2. They are NOT learners. Missing Links believe that they know all that they need to know and therefore don't invest in the skills that would help them out the most. That is not to say that they don't learn at all. They do pick up on environmental learning clues that will help them survive in the business jungle, just not on skills that move them up the leadership evo ladder. They will attend a webinar, but will spend their time doing other things while the webinar is on. They will purchase the books that are considered great leadership books, but will only read a summary and then place the book prominently on a shelf. They spend very little time in learning about the people that they work with. They avoid learning things that force them to get in touch with their relational capabilities.
3. They are withholders of information. The have taken Sir Francis Bacon's quote, "Knowledge is Power" to an extreme. They believe that if they restrict the knowledge of others then they will remain powerful and even gain in their power. They gather information that is needed to conduct one's job and then refuse to distribute the information. One of the strangest

examples of this was when a CEO of a multi-location company had created a vision and a mission and then refused to share it with his team. When questioned, in front of me, by the COO as to how anyone was supposed to know what he wanted if he never told them, the CEO casually responded… "You should have just known me." Really? Really? I had to stifle a laugh as I thought about examples from my own career where I had a regional manager that went out of his way to ensure that his direct reports had the wrong information so that he would look smarter when he knew the right answer. I remember the time that a manager where I worked told an employee when the meeting was and told them the wrong time. I overheard the conversation and asked the manager if she wanted me to let them know when the right time was because the memo I had gotten, as did many others, said one hour earlier. She looked at me and said, "I don't like them. Let them look like a moron for not being there." The mark of the Missing Link is that they continuously try to drag others down so that they look better. They don't build themselves up to look better. They tear others down .

4. They continuously play favorites at work and sometimes even in their families. There is a strong difference between favoring a top performer and playing favorites. Playing favorites denotes that the person who is receiving the favor is doing so without the expectation of performing the job at the highest level. Littered across our country are leaders who really like somebody on the team, but not for legitimate business reasons. Working in a hospital years ago as a consultant, I remember a COO who really liked a young man that worked there. They young man was chronically late, consistently disrespectful to his direct supervisor,

blatantly arrogant, and… untouchable. This leader went so far as to force a contractor to hire the young man when the hospital finally was able to fire him. This way, the young man could still be employed there. Favorites are not expected to be accountable for performance and results. They are generally a problem for anyone who is a top performer and they are often the workplace death of the person showing them favor. As a reminder, it is a great idea to publicly brag about a top performer. It is a phenomenal idea to reward top performers and not poor performers. The logic does not happen with the Missing Link. They think with their lizard brain. They have not evolved as a leader.

5. The Missing Link believes that they are infallible and incapable of being wrong. The clinical definition of this person would likely be Narcissism. In Greek Mythology, Narcissus was a hunter and was the son of a river god and a nymph. He was known for his exceptional beauty. He was so proud and arrogant that he even had a disdain for those that admired him, feeling that they were not worthy of being in his presence. Nemesis, the god of revenge, became angry at Narcissus and lead him to a pool of water where he could see a perfect reflection of himself. He instantly fell in love with the image, yet did not realize that it was simply a reflection. He could not leave the beauty that was before him and he remained at the pool of water, gazing longingly at the image until he died. The story illustrates the leadership death that the Missing Link often faces. When you simply cannot see any faults in yourself, you will eventually kill your own leadership capacity. The Missing Link does not learn from each failure though. They simply find a new pool of water to gaze into and bask in their rightness as a leader.

The Cave Man

Our next leadership stage in the evolutionary process is the Cave Man. The Cave Man has learned some things along the way. They have come to the realization that they are not always right, but have not come to terms with admitting that. They have learned how to get more work done. They use tools, draw pictures, and organize groups. The tools that they use are the people in their organization. Each person is seen as having a purpose for the success of the cave man and for the tribe that they are a part of. Even though this is not as positive of a viewpoint as would be ideal, it is definitely better than the Missing Link. They draw pictures of the possibilities that an employee could achieve. They often use the dangling of great possibilities in front of their employees, but seldom fulfill their end of the bargain and deliver on their promises. They have not fully developed a sense of right and wrong. They see good and bad, but see it more from a "getting away with it" versus "getting in trouble for it" standpoint. They are much more gifted at the use of fear in their pictures of the future and expect people to run from that fear and towards the Cave Man's goal. They did, however, learn a few things from their Missing Link precursors. They learned that you do have to organize people into work teams in order to get anything done in business. They have developed a much stronger sense of the use of pain and pleasure to motivate. There are five characteristics that mark the Cave Man and really make him stand apart.

1. The Troglodyte, or Cave Man, was known for living in a cave. I know that seems very obvious, but it is still true today. The Cave Man leader creates caves or "isolated realities" to live inside of at work. They protect

themselves while pitting tribes (we call them departments or divisions) against each other. They go out of their way to shore up their position at work and to protect themselves by becoming the favorite of their boss. They don't achieve this through performance, but rather through cunning and manipulation. Often, the cave man has something on the tribal leader (boss) that they know will damage their ability to lead the tribe. You can tell when you are in a company with Cave Man leaders, because the departments all believe that they have individual goals and will fight one another on budget, attention, and resources. On the other hand, environments without Cave Man leaders have a unified goal and are all going in the same direction.

2. The Cave Man is much more aggressive about personal success. Unlike the Missing Link, they do learn from their mistakes and continue to attempt to improve their skills. They study the enemy and search for their weaknesses. Cave Man leaders are often very successful in business, because they are capable of a ruthless pursuit of success. They know their landscape (industry), and they know their own skills.
3. The Cave Man carries a club. While the Missing Link was wild and aggressive, the Cave Man is calculated and aggressive. They have learned that appropriately placed fear is what makes the difference. Their approach is generally to use the fear of loss or fear of punishment as the first line of motivation. Their employees, and especially coworkers outside of their cave, are generally nervous around them.
4. The Cave Man values their inner circle. They have a select few that are privy to information that is used to laud over those below them. Those few trusted individuals are still only a tool used to achieve the Cave

Man's purpose of furthering their own agenda. The reality is that every person below the Cave Man is simply a means to an end.

The Cave Man is environmentally adaptive. They have learned to smell fear and compliance in others, and they use that to their advantage. As Machiavelli taught, the ends really do justify the means. They have mastered their skills in reading people and adjusting to get what they need. Their adaptation is about both survival and winning. They will continuously scan their workplace landscape to ensure self-preservation and success.

The Executive Leader

The journey into excellence keeps us moving forward with the evolution from being a cave man to being an executive. The executive is developing their capacity for logic, structure, and systems. Much of their focus is on organizing and systemizing success. They have recognized the reality that having just a few people around you to protect you and build you up isn't enough. The executive leader is at the point of realizing that, in order to be successful, you have to equip people at each level to equip their people so that success can be replicated. So often in business, top leaders will promote a person to the next level and then "hope" for them to magically manifest the skills of leadership at that level. The reality that a talent plan is needed has become evident to the executive leader. The executive leader has developed both a mission and a vision for where they wish to take the organization. They have bought in to the big "why" of their organization. You will know this level of leader because of the fruits they produce in their interactions with others. There are three distinct results that you will see with this type of leader.

- A Systems Approach: Unlike the Missing Link or the Cave Man, the Executive has recognized cause and effect in behavior patterns. At each level, the evolving leader gets smarter and more controlled. The Executive looks at each of the practices in their business and determines what the effect of implementing the behavior/act will be. In their hiring practices, if they are experiencing great turnover, they evaluate the steps of the process that they are using and adapt each step until they get the result that they want. If they are experiencing turnover in only one department, they are astute enough to focus on that department and the leadership behaviors of that departmental leader. When people leave their organization, they invite open and honest feedback in exit interviews. They do not look at problems and simply say that they have always been there and always will be. They take action to put systems in place in order to eliminate the possibility of the problem continuing. Like the Cave Man, they learn from their experiences. Unlike the Cave Man, they do something lasting about it. You will see systems in place in any organization where Executive Leadership is present.
- A Talent Map: The Executive Leader has learned that people have to be developed BEFORE they are put in the position of leadership. People don't know what they don't know. The mistake that many of the "less evolved" leaders will make is to simply put people in charge without preparing them for that leadership role. The skills required at each next level up are different from the position that a person is in right now. The Executive Leader will assess their top talent and then compare their existing talent pool to their top talent. Once the comparison has been made, systemized development is

put into place to bridge the gaps between where people are and where they need to be in order to succeed. The mark of the Executive Leader is their willingness and desire to develop themselves and their teams in order to continuously build their bench strength. They strive to always have someone ready to move up to the next level in order to achieve greater and greater success.

- Rule by Rules: The one thing that seems to hold the Executive Leader back is their intense desire to rule by the rules. They believe that adding a new rule will fix the problem. They have seen the importance of developing the skills of their people, but often miss the importance of focusing everything on the other person's success. Instead of the right focus on others, they focus on the rules, policies, and procedures. Rules without relationships will most often lead to rebellion. Rules with relationships will lead to compliance. Relationships with rules will lead to engagement. You cannot rule by the rules alone and expect things to stay smooth. The primary focus will have to shift to relationships, which is exactly what the Super Leader does consistently.

The Super Leader

The objective that each of us should have is to become a Super Leader. The Super Leader goes way beyond the capacity for success that the Executive, the Cave Man, or the Missing Link have ever had the potential to achieve. To evolve means to learn from your environment and your challenges, to grow from those challenges, and to become a better and more capable person because of that growth. Our objective should be to evolve into the best version of our self. In order to do this, we will have to face challenges, learn, grow, adapt, and succeed. We will have to struggle and overcome. There isn't a person out there that has succeeded without overcoming struggles a few times in life. The greater the challenge you overcome, the greater the capacity you develop for success. This means that we should not be upset about facing challenges. Instead, we should be inspired to work harder and smarter because we know we will be better in the end.

There are three basic components of the Super Leader. All Super Leaders exhibit these focus areas as an extension of themselves. Just like you learned in the beginning of this book, these characteristics keep the Super Leader in rhythm. They don't have to think about doing these things. They are simply a part of who they are. The Super Leader will focus on others before themselves. They will invest in themselves and their personal growth every month because that is how they help others to achieve success. And, they are Master Communicators who are capable of bringing out the best in others.

1. Other Centered: Being other centered means that your thought processes and decision making center around other people. This is not to say that you always put yourself in situations that are not good for you. It simply means that you filter your decisions through the lens of what will help the other person become more successful. The concept of "servant leadership" says that we should ask people... "How may I serve you?" Being other centered is not just about doing things for others. Instead, it is really about helping others to be truly successful. In order for others to be successful, they will have to be accountable first. The Super Leader searches for ways to help others become

more effective and more accountable in their endeavors. Consider the ways in which you filter your decisions. Are you simply doing things for others to make their life easier? Or, are you helping others do for themselves so they will be successful long-term?

2. Always Growing: You can only develop people to one level below where you are. The Super Leader fully understands that they must ALWAYS develop themselves in order to have more to offer their teams. There will never be a time that any of us knows everything. We have something to learn and a new way to grow. One of the best challenges that I ever accepted as a leader was to read a new book for personal development every month. For 15 years, and counting, I have read a new book for personal development each month. This has led to me participating in dozens of seminars and training programs by these authors. The more that I learn, the more that I realize I need to learn. Our educational system creates the false assumption that receiving a degree means that you know all that you need to know. The reality is that your education is the starting point, but not the ending point of your growth. The Super Leader will grow and learn consistently for the rest of their lives.
3. Master Communicator: The Super Leader realizes that the quality of their leadership is dependent on the quality of their communication. We spend more time in business listening than any other aspect of communication. This means that the Super Leader is a skilled listener. They understand that listening is about being focused on the person that they are with, responding non-verbally to the

speaker, asking questions, and feeding back what they heard to ensure clarity of the message. A master communicator focuses on getting their message across through the effective use of non-verbal communication, employing proper tone, pitch, inflection, expression, and body language. As you learned in the chapter on Hypnotic Communication, being a master communicator is an active process. A master communicator realizes that there is always something new for them to learn and they will always focus on their growth as a communicator.

5 LEADERSHIP MAGNETISM
ATTRACTING TOP PERFORMERS TO YOUR TEAM

The best leaders in this world are those who seem to have a magnetic pull that draws others to them. They seem to have a pull that makes other great performers and leaders want to learn from them and orbit around them, held in place by their personal magnetism. –Jody Holland

Napoleon Hill indicated in his book, Think And Grow Rich (Hill, Think And Grow Rich, 1938), that the only thing that could not be taught related to personal success was the concept of personal magnetism. Throughout history, people have referred to this characteristic in various ways. Some have called it charisma. Others have referred to it as mojo. Some even call it your groove. Whatever you want to call it, it can be defined in basically the same way. It is an energy that draws others to you. That energy has often been thought of as illusive. While I will agree that it takes definite focus to master, it can be truly mastered as a leader. What won't work is the idea of faking it. To develop leadership magnetism, you must modify three key components of who you are at your core. Once these three components of you are modified and you fully embrace the growth that accompanies the evolution, then and only then will you have that magnetism that draws others to you.

The three components are simple to discuss, but require completely letting go of old beliefs in order to master them. These components that must be mastered are:

1. Right Beliefs
2. Right Thoughts
3. Right Behavior Patterns

In order to learn the right pattern of beliefs, you will have to be even more willing to unlearn your existing pattern of beliefs. The thing that all truly great leaders have in common is a specific set of beliefs. The following beliefs are what I have gleaned from my two decades of working with executives and great leaders from a wide variety of organizations.

1. You must believe in an attitude of love. I am not saying that you have to grow a beard, stop showering, and tell everyone that they are groovy. That's already been tried in the 60's and it didn't get us where we needed to be. What I am saying is that you must every person and every situation with a sincere desire to find the good in

them. When you look at other people, you have to see them as equal beings. You cannot have prejudice or hate or envy or jealousy or lust or any other destructive belief about that person. An attitude of love looks at the person and sees not just who they are but also who they can be. This belief about the best in others will enable you to see the good that exists in the midst of the bad. One common misunderstanding about the attitude of love is that it is an attitude of acceptance of everything that comes your way. Love is a positive emotion. However, it is not a dumb emotion. To love everyone is to want the best for everyone. Often times, people cannot achieve their best in their current situation and must be given the opportunity to excel somewhere else. Often times, people will act out to bring down the rest of the team. When that is the case, you must have enough love to protect your team and to use tough love to let that person move on to a place where they can find their happiness.

2. You must believe in the impossible. At one point, the earth was flat, only birds could fly, it was impossible to run a 4-minute mile, and computers could not be carried by a person because they were too large. Over the years, Marconi mastered the ether and created a system for the transmission and reception of radio waves. The iPod made it possible to carry 10,000 Cd's in your pocket. Skype made video calls more than a reality. They became free. YouTube became the largest repository of new and original video content in the world. Leaders who attract people to them are the ones that have a vision of how they will change some aspect of the world by never believing that their ideas are impossible. They push beyond the nay-Sayers and the disbelievers. The forge through the waters of change

with such voracity that they leave a wake that pulls people along. When one person believes in the impossible and knows, without any doubt, that they will achieve it, others have to follow because we all want to witness miracles.

3. Great leaders believe in a bonded tribe. They don't create an environment where one department or division is competing with the others for budget dollars or resources. They create a one-tribe, one-goal mentality. Even if your tribe is broken up into 25 divisions, every divisions goals flow from the overarching goal of the tribe. The great leader sets the course with a compelling vision. Once the course is set, then, and only then, the rest of the tribal leaders begin setting support goals that will drive the entire tribe in the same direction. As Ralph Waldo Emerson so eloquently put it, "No member of a crew is praised for the rugged individuality of his rowing." Unless every member of the tribe is focused on the singular vision of the great leader, the tribe will not succeed. The great leader believes that their job is to spend time building relationships and helping to facilitate the bonding of tribal leaders who will spend time bonding the tribal members.
4. Super leader believe that the organization is organic and evolutionary. A living organism has strong needs for coordinated communication. Every aspect of it is connected. If you hurt one division of the organism, it affects every other component of the organism. For an organic system to live, it must have a clearly defined system of signals and messages. It must have a highly coordinated central communication system. The super leader could be considered to be the energy or the fabric that controls the communication pulses that travel,

almost instantaneously, from one business unit to another. The organic organization doesn't function in a mechanistic manner. It has a flow and an energy about it. When the central communication system is functioning as it should, it not only keeps people connected, it makes them better and better. The organization itself becomes stronger with every challenge that it collectively overcomes. It sees the challenges of business as opportunities to prove its collective worth and to expand its capacity. It learns from challenges and prepares contingency plans for the next time a challenge occurs. The leader must believe in the life force of the organization. They must believe in the glorious purpose that the organization will fulfill. They must believe that the change that they are working on through perfectly coordinated efforts will result in new ways to serve and protect their customers and their employees. Because the organization is organic, it is not governed by rules. Instead, it is governed by the symbiotic relationship of all of the business units. Each one focused on the success of themselves as well as the success of the others. Each unit understands that success is only possible through the success of the whole. The super leader keeps those beliefs alive and coordinates the efforts of the units for the benefit of the whole.

5. Super leaders believe in the balanced success of their teams. They know that for a person to achieve true success in life, they must achieve success in all of the domains of life. Inside of the work domain, success can only be achieved when the work is both fulfilling and empowering. This means that each employee must feel a sense of engagement in the efforts that they provide. People are engaged when they embrace the vision, feel

they are a part of an organic movement, and see that they are valued as a person. Super leaders want their people to have great relationships at home. They want them to be financially successful. They want them to have a spiritual connection that fulfills them. They want them to take care of their physical well-being. When these domains of life are supported and encouraged, and the super leader creates a cultural environment that inspires people to want to give their best, that is when balanced success has been achieved.

The second component of Leadership Magnetism is that of Right Thought. Right thought focuses on the thought patterns and thought origins of the super leader. If the beliefs of a person could be considered the roots of success, then the thoughts would be the nutrients. Based on the way that we think, we attract certain outcomes to us. Having the right beliefs will set you on the path towards the right thoughts but it is not the only aspect of attracting fantastic people to your organization. Super leaders know that they must build their positive thoughts and their positive focus. This is done by putting the right information into their minds on a daily basis and by surrounding themselves with right thinking people. The following are the thought focuses of super leaders that will draw top performers into the organization.

1. Failure is not optional! It is required! Magnetic leaders see every mistake, every failure, as an opportunity to learn and grow. They ask the three key questions that turn mess ups into learn ups. They ask for an explanation of the steps that were followed in order to achieve the results that were achieved. They ask at which point the person could have made a different choice. And finally, they ask what the person will put

into place for the future to ensure the right outcome. By asking these three questions, the super leader guides the individual into a recovery and helps them to see that failure is only failure when you give up. The truth about doing something wrong is that the person now knows a great way never to attempt that again. By taking on that mindset, failure doesn't crush people. It will instead make them stronger!

2. Successful people are built through behavioral affirmation and appreciation. They are not built by attempting to make them afraid for their jobs or their position or any other aspect of fear-mongering. When a person does something that is great that the leader wants more of, the super leader will take time to affirm the person by stating the behavior that they witnessed, the way that seeing them perform that behavior made the leader feel, and what the measurable positive effect of the behavior was. Those three components solidify the future implementation of that behavior by the employee. As humans, we crave affirmation. We wear the right clothes so that people will compliment us. We push for more likes and attention in social media to make ourselves feel better. We naturally want to turn positive attention on ourselves. A magnetic leader will understand the need that people have for affirmation and will continuously think of ways to provide that to them when they perform.
3. Magnetic leaders think yes or yes scenarios. We crave time with people who make us feel that the world is a great place to be. We go to the movies to see a struggle that ends in a happy ending. We listen to music that helps us get in touch with our emotions. We watch sports in the hopes that our team will be victorious. Too many people who are in charge of others spend

their time looking for the no or no scenarios. They want to see others fail. They look for what is wrong with every situation. They look for why things won't work. The magnetic leader creates the opportunity to dream and to dream big. When faced with a challenge, they look for the win for themselves and the other party that is involved. They try to eliminate barriers to success for their people and they make every effort to get their team to see the yes opportunities that are all around them.

4. Magnetic leaders are always in motion. They are people of action. They do not wait for something to happen for them. They make something happen at every turn. In order to make a change in the world that leaves this place better than we found it, the magnetic leader knows that they must choose to take action. Given the options between doing nothing and doing something, the magnetic leader will always do something. Theodore Roosevelt said, "In any moment of decision, the best thing you can do is the right thing, the next best thing is the wrong thing, and the worst thing is nothing." People do not follow a person who takes no action because there is no motion. It is only when a person is in action that others have the opportunity to follow. It is only when a person is moving forward that they create a path for others to follow.
5. And finally, leaders have a definite purpose. The driving thought that consumes the magnetic leader is that of the ultimate purpose that he or she has. They see the purpose in every action they take. They think about their purpose without ceasing. They think about their purpose so often that it comes out in their speaking without them even realizing that it is there at times. They have taken their belief in their ultimate goal

and translated that into an unwavering focus. This definite purpose keeps every other aspect of their thoughts on the right path. It fills them with joy and expectancy at every turn. It builds them up and gives them the toughness that is needed to withstand the blows of struggle that come their way. It also equips them with the unwavering focus that is needed to inspire and re-inspire a team of people who need to believe in someone who believes ultimately in something. Their definite purpose becomes the thing that they know absolutely. It is the thought that makes them into an unstoppable force in life, in business, and in drawing others to them. Followers flock to a person who knows exactly who they are and exactly where they are going. This is so rare in thought, that I would argue that 98% of all people have not developed this definiteness. In order to have your definite purpose become a part of you, you must recite it every morning and every night. You must tell others about it and shape your actions based on the fulfilling of the purpose.

The final of the three components of the magnetic leader is that of Right Action. Right action is the behavioral makeup of the magnetic leader. Right action can be seen in all successful people When backed by right thoughts and right beliefs, the results that are achieved are permanent. When exhibited on their own, without the right thoughts and beliefs to back them up, right actions will yield only temporary results. Followers will figure out the truth about the leader if their thoughts and beliefs don't back up the things that they are doing to achieve success. Five key actions of the magnetic leader are…

1. Magnetic leaders communicate clearly. One of the great challenges that followers face is that of truly understanding the expectations of their leader. Many people who are in charge will grunt out their orders like a missing link but will never take the time to lay out their expectations. Just as important, the super leader will take the time to define the roles of each of her or his team members. They will also take the time to provide feedback on a regular basis and according to the needs of the individual. This doesn't mean that they are spending inordinate amounts of time chit-chatting with their team. What it does mean is that the super leader will clearly establish expectations and deadlines for projects. They will communicate their observations of the project throughout the process. And, they will evaluate the effectiveness of the person in the project, offering consultative advice on how they can continuously improve. They are both tactful and honest in the evaluations, keeping the focus on how to help the employee grow and evolve.
2. Magnetic leaders model the behaviors that they want from others. The "Golden Rule" is to do unto others as you would have them do unto you. Today's super leader takes it even one step farther. Do as you would have others do. This goes beyond how you treat others and displays the level of focus, success, and drive that you desire in the people that you lead. To live as an example of success, personal development, and continuous growth is the responsibility of the super leader. Every day, as you start your day, you should remind yourself that the way in which you behave is the way in which others will follow. Be the leader that you desire in others.

3. Magnetic leaders are learners. They inspire others to want to learn by investing in themselves, as well as their teams. They don't send others to training while believing that they have learned all that they need to know. They realize that there is always something new to learn and they show up to training programs with a great attitude in order to demonstrate that the training is important. One of the most critical aspects of creating a leadership culture is that of development. Just like the second point in leadership behaviors, you must set the example for others to follow. Invest in yourself and both you and your team will benefit. Leaders have big libraries. Followers have big TV's. The most successful people that I have met invested more each year in their learning than they did in their entertainment. Which are you investing in?
4. Magnetic leaders associate. They go out of their way to associate with people who have already exhibited the beliefs, thoughts, and actions of a great leader. They seek out opportunities to learn from other great leaders. When developing their relationships, they consider the behaviors of the people they are around and focus on spending time with people that behave like the leader they want to be. They do not associate with the drifters of the world. They avoid people who do not operate with a definite purpose and a chief aim in life. The leader who wants to move from the stage of the Executive Leader to that of the Super Leader will find as many Super Leaders as possible to hang out with. They will build their relational rolodex around people who are living the life that the magnetic leader desires. They don't seek to sponge off of the great leaders. Instead, they seek to find ways to serve them and through that service, they learn from them.

5. Magnetic leaders coach for success. They invest time in knowing their people and will push those people towards higher and higher levels of success. Great coaches know the capacity of their players. Great leaders know the potential of their teams. They employ assessment tools and evaluation systems to unlock the hidden aspects of their teams. They study the individuals on their teams so that they will be prepared to help them evolve to each next level up. Because the magnetic leader is growing themselves, they always have something of value to offer their team. Coaching is the day in, day out, never-ending process of being connected with one's team for the purposes of helping them succeed at higher and higher levels.

When you mix the right beliefs with the right thoughts with the right actions, you have a formula for the right results. Simply changing the outward behaviors without first changing the patterns of belief and thought will not produce a permanent result. That would be the equivalent of setting an orange in an apple tree and waiting for it to switch and start growing oranges. It may hold the 1 orange there for a while, but it will never change itself. In order to get oranges instead of apples, you must change the roots. New root equals new fruit. Old root equals old fruit. If you want the new result in your life, you must change the aspect of your life that was causing the old result.

Belief + Thought + Action = Result

Right Belief + **Right** Thought + **Right** Action = **Right** Result

6 LEADING WITH CLARITY

BECOMING CLEAR ABOUT YOUR PURPOSE

"He who reigns within himself, and rules passions, desires, and fears, is more than a king." --John Milton

As young people are trained up in the ways of business, they are taught to be certain, even absolute, about the direction that they will take their companies. They are taught that to be anything other than certain is a sign of weakness. As you read this, I would like for you to think about some of the lessons that you were taught as a young person. Think about the messages that were passed on to you from your parents/guardians. For example, what were you taught about Democrats or Republicans? What were you taught about coaches? What were you taught about big choices like religion or spirituality? What were you taught about the value of a life? What were you taught about gun control, freedom of thought, or the role of a certain gender at home, or work for that matter? Think back to why you have the beliefs that you have right now about each of the important things in life. Are those your beliefs, or were they the beliefs that you accepted from people in positions of authority?

I remember asking myself that question when I was 18 years old and on my own, sort of, at college. Growing up the son of a preacher, I was taught early on what religion is all about. I also had my own opinions about what people who were pious/overly-religious were like. I was questioning whether or not I believed what I was taught to be certain about. I didn't know if I wanted to be religious or not. I had seen how mean people in the church could be to the pastor and the pastor's family. I had seen my father diffuse situations, calm people, make peace, and never give up on his faith in the midst of it. I had seen some great people in church as well. I had seen people that cared for us as a family, wanted us to have good things, and brought us some of the best baking in the world! My life consisted mainly of going to church and learning the lessons that were taught there. Once I was on my own, I had to decide whether or not those were my truths or someone else's truths. It may sound crazy, but I remember thinking that I wished I had been a lost soul who found God on my own, so that I would know for sure that it was my choice.

I want you to think about the examples that you have seen in leadership positions, as well as what you were taught about leadership in business. Have you seen people that were absolute about being right, regardless of the consequences? Have you seen people that were so strong in their convictions that others, who knew they were wrong, would simply go along with the leader and not say what they were thinking? I have seen example after example of what it was like for people to lead with certainty, but not really have any clarity. I have seen leaders that HAD to be right, but were never clear about where they were going.

An example of this is the behaviors that leaders choose to exhibit in front of their teams and in their communications with others. I have seen leaders push so hard to reach a goal that they demonstrated that they really didn't care about the people. They were certain about where the company was going, but they were not clear about what was actually going to get them there. It is the moment of clarity that counts. It is the choice to be clear, instead of just having to be right in the circumstances that we face in business. Having clarity in your leadership means being clear on what is going on in our businesses, as well as keeping watch on our people. It means knowing ourselves to the point of knowing when to get out of our own way, so that the organization can succeed.

There are three key areas that we must focus on in order to become and remain clear in our endeavors. They are purpose, process, and flow. By being completely honest in each of these areas, we will be able to define the right future for ourselves. As individuals, as companies, as non-profits, as athletes, we need to be able to master the "Keys2Clarity" that are outlined in this chapter. We must also be able to understand when we are falling prey to certainty, that is not backed with clarity.

Purpose

The first thing that we must do is define our purpose. There are several ways in which we can accomplish this. However, the following model is what I have found to be most effective in ensuring that our organizations are truly headed in the right direction. The first step is to answer the following questions…

1. Who is my customer? People often rattle off a list of customers that they have when this question is asked. They say that their employees, other departments, the direct consumer, the indirect consumer, or several other entities are their customer. You have to be able to define the ONE customer that you truly serve. When your attention is divided too many times, you will not be able to serve anyone very well. Dividing your attention, even in half, yields improper results. Fill in the blanks below to begin truly understanding who your primary customer is.

   __________________ is the person/group that I must have in order to keep doing business. This is the person that keeps my business going and that benefits from what it is that we offer.

   __________________ is the person/group that will bring me more paying customers, donors, or other revenue sources.

2. The second question that you must answer has to do with the need that your business satisfies, or the gap that you fill. If you cannot define the need that you take care of, then you are not likely taking care of any needs. If you supply employers with qualified job seekers, then

state that. If you provide customers with high quality pet food, or you provide quality clothing to retailers for the purpose of them and you making a profit, state that. Take a few minutes to write out in two sentences or less… What need does our product/company/organization satisfy?

____

____

____

____

3. This is a very important question, and one that is very difficult for most people to answer. How will you know when you are successful? The vast majority of business owners that I have coached over the years wanted to be in business. That was as far as they had gone in creating clarity for their future. They didn't have a definition of success, or they had a definition that they accomplished and never thought to create a bigger definition of their success. Your vision and definition will evolve over the years, but it is essential that you have both. If you don't have either of them, you will find yourself disappointed, and often even depressed, because there seems to be no meaning to your work. So, take a few minutes to write out exactly what your life will look like once you have achieved success in this endeavor called business. You want to make sure it is something that can be attained. You also have to make sure that it can be measured and tracked. Your definition will need to contain both an accurate description and the components for measuring

success. This is your definition of success! What others think is not relevant for the purposes of this exercise. Simply write out your thoughts here. You can always modify it down the road.

The things that I will achieve and can measure to demonstrate success in this endeavor are:

____

____

____

____

____

____

4. What values will govern your actions as you achieve these goals? People will work harder and longer for a values driven purpose than they ever will for money. If money is the only value that governs your actions, you will have very few friends and find it very difficult to convince others that you can be trusted. You need to define the way in which you measure your actions. If you know what the primary values are that govern you and your endeavors, then you will make your choices based on those values. Values are those tricky items that we don't often define, but we do ALWAYS live by. You can see a list of value words at: www.leadershipevo.com/values.html. Take the list of value words and pick 20 words that you identify with

emotionally when you think of the word and your business. Write those words in the table below and then follow the instructions that follow the box in order to get to your top 3 values.

Name of Value	Why Is This Important?
1.	
2.	
3.	
4.	
5.	
6.	
7.	
8.	
9.	
10.	
11.	
12.	
13.	

14.	
15.	
16.	
17.	
18	
19.	
20	

Now that you have listed out 20 value words that mean something to you or your team, if you are working together, the next step is to begin the elimination process. As a team, or on your own, you will want to go through and begin eliminating one value at a time that means the least to you. Most teams find it very difficult to agree, once you get down to about seven (7) values. It is critical that you continue eliminating value words until you get down to only three value words. These will be the three values that you and your team would be absolutely willing to fight for, to give up sleep over, and to make sacrifices to keep intact. Do not table the discussion. Use a specific meeting just for choosing the 3 absolute values.

5. Finally, for this section, you need to define how people will know who you are and what you are all about. You have to define your medium for connection with others.

In other words, how will you connect with people to ensure that they understand your purpose? If you have the best purpose in the world, but people don't know about it, what does it matter? You won't change anything without the connection. Some people tell their story through direct connection. Some people build their brand through success association. Some people focus on changing the way the world works in their corner of the universe and attracting people to them. Whatever your approach, you have to decide what the medium and mode will be. If you don't, you will find yourself running around throwing your message at anyone and everyone. This generally does not accomplish anything. It annoys people! However, it doesn't create change. Facebook is wrought with examples of people who are spewing their beliefs and belittling anyone who has a dissenting belief. I have not seen a single person, who just got slammed for their beliefs, come back and say… "Wow, I never thought of that. I am going to change my beliefs starting right now." All I have witnessed is the escalation of disagreement. I would argue that most people have not changed their opinions because of a Facebook post, particularly on politics and religion. Your objective has to be clear on how you will get your message out and who your target audience is. "Everyone" is not the correct answer. Not everyone will want what you have and that is too broad of a target anyway. An example would be that I will focus my message on entrepreneurs that are within the first 3 years of business and have found themselves stuck at less than $500,000 in annual revenues. I will connect with them through small business development centers, chamber meetings, and networking groups, by delivering a speech on how to bust through business plateaus as a business owner. Once you are clear on how you will connect with them, you may find that sponsoring the seat cushions for a volleyball tournament at your local junior high makes no sense. On the other hand, if you are a chiropractor, then the seat cushions for junior high volleyball tournaments is a perfect idea. With clarity, you only do the things that actually move you toward your stated goal.

Process

Once you have solidified the "WHY" of your organization, project, or personal leadership, the rest is a matter of systems. In pushing yourself to lead with clarity, you have to be able to move past your ego. In the chapter on Leadership Styles, you learned about the qualities of a Super Leader. You learned that you have a vision, clearly communicated goals, a clear grasp on the strengths and weaknesses of your team members, and a full understanding of your resources. During the process portion of leading with clarity, you will employ all of those characteristics. Sun Tzu, in The Art of War (Tzu, 2007) discusses that a great strategy with little tactics is the calm before the victory, while great tactics with little strategy is the noise before the defeat.

In this section, you will learn each of the following…

- Positioning The Vision
- Clarifying The Strengths of Your Team
- Laying Out Clear Metrics For Success
- Defining Success Tasks
- Appropriate Allocation of Resources

The vision that you have for the team and for the organization keeps the "Why" in front of your team members and helps to maintain their motivation. In Herzberg's 2-Factor Theory of Motivation, he explains that there are intrinsic and extrinsic motivators, or hygiene and maintenance factors. The intrinsic factors center around the emotional engagement that a person feels in dealing with their teams. People have an innate need to be a part of something bigger than themselves. They want to belong and know that they are bringing meaning to this world. People want to be recognized, at least in their own minds, for doing something great. The vision that we have, backed by sincere appreciation for the achievement of positive results, will keep our teams excited and moving full-steam ahead. Your vision is what you start every staff meeting with. Your vision is mounted on the walls of your office and plastered on your website, your social media, and your business cards. It must be simple and easy to understand. It must become an extension of who you are as a person. When you and your vision become aligned, you will be where you are supposed to be. It will become part of your soul. Moving your leadership capacity to the highest level means being the person that this world needs, that your employees need, and that you need for yourself. Until you ARE that person, the world doesn't change. So answer this right now, If you could do anything in the world and you knew that you could not fail, what would you do? Remember, you know without reservation that you cannot fail. Take a moment to write that out on the lines below. Make it simple and precise.

___

Now answer this… If every job in the world paid exactly the same, what job would you do?

And finally, what is it that you do that brings you joy and energy? What makes you feel that sense of purpose that lightens your heart and inspires your soul?

This exercise helps people to get in touch with the reality of what motivates them. It helps you become clear about your purpose on this earth, your passion, and your true self. A very big part of clarity is to ensure that you are the right leader, with the right team members, at the right time. Having the right people on your team begins with being the right leader right now. If you are that right leader, then cast a vision that will put a dent in the universe, that will change the way in which we conduct ourselves in some aspect of life. A vision should be big, inspiring, and fulfilling for you and for your team. You need to know the action, the result, the value justification, and the why. If you have those four components in your vision, you will have people lining up to follow you to victory.

As you evaluate the strengths of your team, you will need to first understand fully who they are. One of the best ways to do this is by assessing their personality. There are a number of tools on the market that can accomplish this for you. The key is to pick one, learn the ins and outs of it, and then capitalize on the information that it gives you. By understanding the personality and behavioral makeup of a person, you will be more fully prepared to position your team members in the right roles for success. It is also important to remember that you don't want your team to lack diversity in their personality makeup. In the chapter on Leadership Magnetism, we discussed the manner in which leaders attract top talent to them in order to make the team strong. We also defined that talent must be diverse. You must have people that have a diverse skillset from one another. Imagine a football team where everyone was good at throwing, but nobody was good at catching. That would not make for a very successful team. We need each person to be able to play their parts. The four basic breakout areas that you should focus on are:

1. The Communicator – You need someone who is creative and inspiring. This person will be the cheerleader of the group. They will keep the team going, dreaming, and scheming, until they finally reach victory. This person should be positive, outgoing, not afraid to be wrong, and driven to see the possibilities.
2. The Competitor – You need someone who is big picture in their thought and absolutely hates for his or her team to lose. They will push people to be their best, work their hardest, and strive for something a little

higher than before. They will continuously measure their team against itself. This person is the reason that the team makes one more call, one more presentation, one more deal.

3. The Cooperator – You need someone who enjoys working behind the scenes and wants to keep relationships positive. This person will go out of their way to ensure that the end user of your product or service is very satisfied. They avoid conflict and serve as the peacemaker. They keep the team calm and work for team agreement. They are fantastic at doing the work.
4. The Coordinator – You need someone who is good with the details and loves making sure that the schedule is kept. This person is easy to recognize, because they will color-code their notes, their filing, etc. They will know the schedule, know who is suppose to do what, and make sure that everyone stays informed of the deadlines and metrics. They are fantastic at coordinating responsibilities.

You will have combinations of each of these people on your team. The critical thing to keep in mind is that you must have someone that can function in each of the four modes, in order to achieve the success you desire. Some people can switch modes when necessary. If you have a small team, you will want to ensure that they are capable of adapting.

You have to have a clear picture of how you will measure youractivity as well as your results. The metrics with which any team is measured should be understood from the outset. The metrics that you lay out should have three key components.

1. They should be easy to understand. Too many people build complicated measurement systems that simply bog down employees and don't really get you the results that you are looking for. The first rule is to keep it simple. If you don't understand it, they won't either.
2. They should be readily available. You need to publish how you are doing as a team. People need to be able to see the results that they are getting, or not getting. By keeping the tracking in front of every person in your company on a regular basis, you can pull your team toward the goal.
3. They must be celebrated. The metrics should be a cause for celebration, not a cause for disgust. When presented correctly as a Super Leader, you will inspire people to push themselves toward the marks and you will lead them to victory. Every time you reach a target, or a sub-goal, you have to celebrate. One of my early employees and I used to do what we called "the happy dance of joy" every time we closed a new deal. We looked like goofballs, but we were happy and we were celebrating victory! People will lose interest in success very quickly, if the victories are not celebrated.

Defining the tasks of success is equally as important as the other aspects of the process. Too many people fill their days with activities that do not lead to success at their chosen tasks. One of my friends refers to that as dang-infernal-tinkering. That is doing things that make you look and feel busy, but never accomplish much of anything. The easy way to tell if you are doing the tasks of success or not is this… Are you getting closer to fulfilling the vision and goals of the company on a daily basis? If you look at your day and answer no, then change what you are doing. As you define the tasks that fit with this model, you need to keep that list limited. There are never more than five (5) daily tasks that will bring you success. If you have a list of 23 things to do every day that will bring you success, you really have a list of daily frustrations. Most positions really only have 3 things per day that will bring them ultimate success. A simple exercise is to list out the top 3 to 5 things that you do that absolutely move you closer to your vision and your goal. You will do this on the left hand side of the chart that follows. You can only have 5 or fewer on the list, so be very selective. On the right side of the chart, you will write out all of the other things that you do during a day. The key to keeping the process flowing is to ALWAYS start on the left. If you do all of the things on the left before you do any of the things that are on the right, you will be successful.

My Top Tasks For Success	Everything Else That I Do
1.	
2.	
3.	
4.	
5.	
NO MORE	
NO MORE	
NO MORE	

NO MORE	
NO MORE	

The appropriate allocation of resources is the final component of keeping clarity in the process. Everything that you have in business can be seen as a resource or a roadblock. It is a resource for moving toward your goals and vision when used correctly. It is a roadblock when it prevents you from moving toward your goals and vision. You have to take inventory of your resources regularly to ensure that you are using them to their fullest capacity. When I am leading team building programs on ropes courses, I always lay out the resources that the team has at their disposal. They always have the element or challenge that they are on, their creative minds, the team of people that they are working with, and the fresh air around them. It is slightly humorous when presented to them, but the point is the same. If they are not focused on what they have to work with, they will often not work with the things that matter the most. Your people are your greatest resource. They are the creativity, the drive, the work, and the inspiration behind the success of your organization. Make sure to count them among your greatest resources. You may have other things like your reputation, your market position, your backing, or any number of things. Make a few notes here about what you see your resources to be. In fact, list five resources that you have at your disposal that will help you achieve the grand vision that you have set before your team.

____

____

____

____

____

Never forget that these resources are always at the ready for you. They are there to help you, support you, and make you successful. Use them. Value them. Appreciate them. They are your lifeline.

Flow

The final component of Leading With Clarity is the flow, or rhythm of success. To keep in rhythm, you must be able to kick start that rhythm with your team. Success, just like leadership, is simply a perpetual motion that, once started, propels you forward with ever-decreasing effort. When the same amount of effort is applied, the growth and success of the team accelerates. Just like priming a pump to get a motor going, the use of the right methodologies will jump start your leadership. There are two things that you need to do in order to get the leadership movement started, one is to maintain the motion, and the other is to accelerate it.

The Jump Start

The use of process mapping and reverse scheduling will start the engine of the leadership machine. A process map is more than just workflow. It is designed to bring meaning to each aspect of the activities of success that you are doing. The process map demonstrates to the team how each of the components of your vision fit together and what you are ultimately going to accomplish together. A disjointed vision doesn't inspire action. It is only when the team being together is greater than all of the individuals separately that you find success. They only operate as a well oiled machine when they understand what all of the parts are for and how they fit together. You can use almost any mind-mapping program to lay out the process. Visio™ is one of the more popular ones from Microsoft®. To be fair to Apple®, iThoughts HD™ is a mind-mapping program for the iPad. It is cheap and easy to learn, but has fewer functions than Visio™. What you use is less relevant than the fact that you do use a map. Once your map is made, you will need to create a timeline for success. Reverse scheduling lays out the amount of time required for each success activity and the target date for its completion or attainment. If your vision calls for reaching 100,000 people with your message, and it takes an average of 1 minute of effort to reach each person, then you need 100,000 minutes of time to reach the goal. Go backwards 100,000 minutes, or 209 full workdays from the target date for success and that is your full-time starting point. If you can only spend four hours per day on it, then you will have to go back 418 days from the target success date. The point is to put a number to the amount of time it will take, and then to map it backwards from the date of success. This helps to ensure that you allocate your time resource appropriately.

Once you have a process map and have planned the time needed, going backwards from the date of success, you have to keep things in motion. Most of the roadblocks that exist, center around the engagement of your teams. This means that you need to have a plan in place for ensuring the emotional stability of the team. One of the easiest things that you can do is to use your process map and break down the big goals into incremental and measureable, small goals, along the path. These small goals should be celebrated publicly. This public recognition of forward momentum keeps people focused on the momentum. It is the demonstration of appreciation through sincere and precise affirmations that helps to keep your team inspired. Describe the behaviors that lead to the incremental goal success. Describe the positive emotions that the success brings you. Finally, describe the positive effects of meeting that goal. You need your teams to keep looking to the next target, and ultimately, to the final target. Fear creeps in when we, as leaders, focus on the negative too much. We need to remember that people are more positively motivated by reinforcements, than by threats or emotional pain. When people do experience fear of failure, go back to the process, the vision, and focus. F.E.A.R. is false expectations appearing real. Set proper expectations and focus on success tasks to keep fear at bay and success as the focal point.

In conclusion, we create flow when we create rhythm. Rhythm is the harmonious functioning of the team. Success, just like failure, has its own rhythm. Nothing breeds success better than success. The reason that leaders accomplish more and more in this life is because every success builds off of the last one. If you find your team in a negative rhythm, then you have to break the cycle by bringing them back to their definite purpose. You must be clear on why the team exists. You must be clear on who you are as a leader in order to do that. Clarity creates rhythm, and rhythm always supersedes certainty. If you wake up every day and go to work to ensure that the vision you have for your business, your department, your family, or your life is the first thing that you see and the last thing that you do every day, then the rhythm will follow you. Discipline to do the tasks of success consistently every day is what creates that perpetual motion that keeps you in harmony with where you want to take your team.

7 A CULTURE OF ACCOUNTABILITY
SOLID PEOPLE ARE ENGAGED PEOPLE

The word "accountable" originated in the mid 14th century and meant "to be called to account" or "to answer for." Ghandi said, "It is wrong and immoral for one to try to escape the consequences of one's acts."

How many times in life have we been given the example of a person trying to get away with a wrong-doing? How many celebrities have hired high powered lawyers to convince a jury that they were not really guilty? How many people have we seen in this world that are not responsible for their actions because they had a bad childhood, or their 2nd grade teacher was mean to them? How many times do we see people say things like, "I had to turn out bad because my life has been bad." The bigger question is, how many times have you tried to make up justifications, or excuses, for your behaviors? It is wrong and immoral. Those are powerful worlds from Ghandi. We look into our lives and we see things that we wish were not there. We see things that we know we shouldn't see in our own behaviors. We take actions that are contrary to where we want to end up. However, we are the ones who took those actions.

Learning to be accountable and to make good decisions in our lives starts at a very early age. If we wish to create positive accountability in our kids, we need to start from day one teaching them how to be responsible for the choices that they make and the actions that they take. Jason Dorsey, in his book, My Reality Check Bounced (Dorsey, 2007), talks about the fact that older adults in the workplace are upset with young people entering the workplace who don't work as hard or as responsibly as they did. He said in a speech in Atlanta, GA, in July 2013, "If you want kids to be responsible, be responsible for raising responsible kids. After all, you parented us and taught us to be this way." Those are some tough words. He went on to say that every young person makes a choice about who they are going to be, despite the way they were parented, but right parenting makes a tremendous difference.

I bring these things up because I want to make the point that we have a choice. We always have a choice. When we are raising our children, we choose to punish them for doing something wrong, or we choose to let it go. We choose to help guide them through their homework and be responsible, or we choose to do it for them by giving them the answers. We choose to punish them when they disrespect a teacher, or we choose to blame the teacher. The same types of choices are available to us in the workplace. When an employee does not produce the result they were supposed to, we choose to hold them accountable, or we choose to overlook it. When an employee does something fantastic, we choose to recognize them, or we choose to ignore it. From an accountability standpoint, it is us as leaders that will set the culture of the organization. We are the ones that establish the rhythm of success or failure for our people. It is our choices that lead them to believe what their choices are. If we don't take control of our choices, they will not likely take control of their choices. If we don't choose to set the right example, they will normally choose to follow the wrong example. Make no mistake, we are continuously reaping the results of our choices.

There is a truth that is inescapable. The truth is that we are who we are and where we are, because we have chosen to be there. If we wanted to be someone else or somewhere else, we would have to make different choices. As a leader, you have the ability to learn from the mistakes and victories of other people. You have the opportunity to take your company in any direction that you choose. When we embrace our choice, and only once we embrace it, will we see that we were in control the whole time. At whatever level you are at, you are in control of the destiny that exists for you. You are the captain of your soul. I have always loved the poem, "Invictus" because it clearly outlines that we are the masters of our destiny.

Invictus
Out of the night that covers me,
Black as the Pit from pole to pole,
I thank whatever gods may be
For my unconquerable soul.

In the fell clutch of circumstance
I have not winced nor cried aloud.
Under the bludgeonings of chance
My head is bloody, but unbowed.

Beyond this place of wrath and tears
Looms but the Horror of the shade,
And yet the menace of the years
Finds, and shall find, me unafraid.

It matters not how strait the gate,
How charged with punishments the scroll.
I am the master of my fate:
I am the captain of my soul.
--William Ernest Henley

You must be able to answer the following questions correctly every time in order to be personally responsible for your life… "How do I explain what just happened? Is there an internal explanation, or is there an external explanation?" If you explain events in your life internally, then you made a choice, and you will change when necessary. If you explain events in your life externally, then you did not have control, and you will not change. Imagine that you are back in 5th grade. You were supposed to write a book report for English class, and it is due today. You awaken in the morning knowing that you did not complete it. You begin searching your mind for the reason that you did not complete it. You think about the sports that you are involved in, or the stress you have had with your mom and dad fighting, or the fact that you have had lots of stuff going on in life, even as a 5th grader. You decide on the story that you will tell the teacher that will buy you some more time. You tell the teacher that you simply did not have time to finish the book report, because you were not given the support you needed from your parents because of their fighting. The teacher looks at you and remembers her parents fighting when she was young, and tells you that you can have one extra week to complete the assignment. This is the third time that you have gotten away with extending the deadline for your projects at school. You have learned that you are not at fault for not doing your homework. But wait, what you have really learned is that if you blame something external, you can get away with not doing what you are supposed to do. That lesson carries over into high school when you begin playing UIL sports. You simply couldn't get into shape over the summer because of the travel schedule that your family kept. You take it even further into life when you get a professional job. You couldn't get your assignment done that your boss said was important because marketing did not provide you with the figures that you needed in order to complete the assignment. You are now 30 years old and you don't feel that any of the things that have gone wrong in your life are really your fault. Your marriage didn't work out, but really that isn't anyone's fault. People drift apart. You didn't get the promotion that you wanted, but that is really your boss's fault for not realizing your potential. The story could simply go on and on. Make no mistake that every decision you make has a ripple effect. You become a drifter when you choose to not be personally accountable for the choices that you make. You drift through life, allowing the circumstances of life to control you. You don't feel like the captain of your soul or the master of your destiny. You don't feel that way because you handed over the reigns of self-leadership to anyone that wanted them. You gave up control of your own life.

But wait, what if the story went differently? What if in 5th grade you were given an assignment to complete? What if you were asked to write a book report, and it was due today? What if you had started working on the book report the day that it was assigned to you? What if one week after you got your assignment, you were done reading the book and you had made notations throughout the book about things that caught your attention? What if you didn't watch TV for 3 hours a day, and you focused on learning? What if 2 weeks after you had gotten the assignment, and 3 weeks before it was due, you had already written the book report? What if you turned it in early? What if that pattern carried over into your life? What if, in high school, you wanted to run track? What if ,over the summer, you worked out five days a week? What if you put in 1 hour a day of exercise, instead of 1 hour a day of TV or laying around? What if you continued choosing to put in your best effort every day of the off-season? What if, when track season arrived, you were in the best shape of your life? What if you were asked to run the 400 and be on the mile relay team because you were fast and you didn't wear out sprinting all the way around the track? What if you broke several school records, and even went to state and placed? What if you carried that into your professional life and chose to work hard, start work early, and make every effort to be at the top of your game? What would life be like if you never made excuses for your behaviors? What if you lived fully into your potential?

Abraham Maslow said, "If you intentionally become less than you are capable of being, then I warn you, you will be unhappy for the rest of your life."

The vast majority of people that I see are walking through life unhappy, because they have intentionally become less than they were capable of being. They have chosen to externalize their choices. They have not chosen to be accountable. You are a leader. You are an influencer. When you explain things in the right way, taking responsibility for who and where you are, you are much more likely to end up in the right place in life. You will never be able to create accountability in others, unless you first demonstrate accountability yourself. You are the example. You are the leader. The choice is yours. Everyone has the innate need to answer the question, "Why?" Why did this happen? The way in which you answer that question will determine the rest of your life. Choose wisely. If you explain things internally, you will likely take control of the situation and make the necessary changes. If you explain things externally, you will not likely get any better. Things will remain the same, and you will talk about how someone or something else kept you from being who you were meant to be.

Zig Ziglar used to say in his speeches, "You are at the geographical center of the earth. You can get anywhere in the world without traveling more than halfway around the earth from right where you are." You are at that center. You have a choice. Once you make your choice to explain everything in your life based on the choice or series of choices that you made, you will begin making the right series of choices. As you begin to develop the right choice patterns in your people, you will see the results that you achieve in business consistently improve. There is a specific pattern of correction and development that you will need to follow in order to get lasting behavior change and accountability from your people. The last half of this chapter will outline what you will have to choose to do in order to persuade your people to choose the right things for themselves in the future.

Mistakes

Mistakes are often treated very harshly in business. We ask the question, "Why did you do that?" How many times do we really get a legitimate answer though? My guess is that you don't usually get a legitimate explanation. The reason you don't is that 90+% of people don't accept responsibility for their actions. They blame things outside of their choice. Knowing that most of our society is set up as drifters who don't feel responsible for their choices, we have to approach the subject of mistakes differently. We want to create a pattern of responsibility and a system of positive internal explanation. So, we have to ask the right questions to get the right answers. Socrates believed that all knowledge existed in man. He believed that we need only ask the right question to get the right answer. When mistakes happen, and they will happen, you have to begin with stating the situation as you see it. Explain what you are seeing in non-blameful terms. You simply state where you ended up with the result, and what you had intended to achieve as the result. You are defining the gap of where you are versus where you intended to be. The questions that you ask next will determine accountability or blame. So, let's ask the right questions. Those right questions are:

1. Can you walk me through what happened from the beginning?
2. At what point in that process could you have made a different decision that would have gotten us the results that we wanted, instead of the results that we got?
3. What will you put in place so that we get the results we want in the future, and we don't get the current results again?

The key here is that you didn't yell or throw things or behave as "The Missing Link" would have behaved. You behaved as a leader who wanted to get the right results every time would behave. You behaved as a super-leader.

The Conversation

When you are stating the situation and asking these questions, the way in which you present yourself will make a tremendous difference. Your non-verbal signals tell the whole truth of who you are at your core. Your face gives you away, as do your mannerisms while you speak. You want to make sure that you exhibit the following characteristics when you approach the person who needs to be accountable for their behaviors and make a change. Remember, it is your choice to be accountable for your approach.

1. Make warm eye contact. There should not be white showing in your eyes above or below the iris. You should make sure that your eyes are open to the point of showing most of the iris, but not so much that you are showing white above and below your iris. When

you are showing white below your iris, you come across as disillusioned. An aggressive person's eyes will narrow to the point of only showing about half of the iris. Imagine you are open or welcoming. Try to feel that emotion. What does your face look like when you are open and welcoming? That is what you want to display when you are trying to get people to decide to change. The mistake that most people make here is to come across as aggressive or overly disappointed. This puts up a defensive wall between you and the person who needs to change. Your eye contact is supposed to remove the wall, and when done right, it does just that.

2. Make your body language serious, but inviting. You want to be on the same level as the person that you are talking with. It is best not to be facing them directly. Instead, be at a 45-degree angle to them. Don't stand over them or get too close to them. They need their personal space. Refrain from crossing your arms, rubbing your head, or tilting your head back and closing your eyes (yes, people do that). Look at the person, but also glance away at the table or something in between the two of you. The lion-share of your attention should be focused on them. After you make your point about the situation and then ask the question, you will want to lean forward just a little bit to denote that you are ready to listen. It may even be a good idea to have a pen and paper in front of you to take notes about what they say. This way, you can review the steps that they followed and reiterate the place in which they stated that they could have made a different decision. Being able to give feedback to what you heard is critical.
3. Make sure that you shake hands with the person at the end of the conversation. This may seem a little strange to some people, but the non-verbal signal that you are

giving is that you have an agreement about the direction that they will follow in the future. You will end the conversation with restating what they have chosen to do in the future to ensure that the right results are achieved and then standing and extending your hand. You want to have a firm handshake, along with looking them in the eyes. Let them know that you appreciate the choice they are making and you look forward to the positive results. The next piece of this is critical and absolutely cannot be overlooked.

Making The Change Stick

Change only becomes permanent when it is reinforced. The only things in life that stick are the ones that are seen as valuable. The most common mistake that I have seen from executives is to believe that when a person begins doing the right things right, that they don't have to recognize it. After all, wasn't that what they were being paid to do anyway? Here is a truth that has proven to be 100% accurate over the last decade and a half of coaching and training that I have done. <u>If the change is not valued, the change is not permanent.</u> You, as a leader, must be observant of when a person does what you have asked them to do and you must affirm it. You affirm it by using the three components of an appreciative message. Those three components are:

1. Describe the behavior.
2. Describe the positive effect of that behavior on you, the organization, etc.
3. Describe how you feel about the positive behavior.

By having these three components in your appreciation message, you will find that people will go out of their way to exhibit the positive behavior again and again. After all, we are all seeking positive experiences and trying our best to avoid negative ones.

Side note: The three components of a message of appreciation are the same three components that must be present in a confrontation message.

You can step down the frequency in which you recognize the positive or desired behavior over time. In the beginning (week 1), you really do have to recognize the positive behavior daily. You can then step it down to once per week for a month. After a month, you can recognize it once a month for the next six months. After that, the change is simply the norm for that person. The objective was to make the positive change permanent. By following this model, you can do that.

Recapping the main points of this chapter, because it is extremely important that you get these things, remember…

1. You set the tone. The personal accountability that you exhibit will determine, to a large degree, the accountability that you get.
2. The way you communicate determines the response that you get.
3. Mistakes are opportunities for growth when handled correctly. Your response will determine their future behaviors, good or bad.
4. Accountability in others begins with the questions that we ask and the way in which we ask those questions.

5. Stick-ability of change is determined by the leader's reinforcement of positive behaviors.
6. It takes time to make change permanent.
7. Accountability is explaining things in terms of having internal control. Lack of accountability is explained in terms of not having control of circumstances or situations.

8 TRANSFORMATIONAL LEADERSHIP
MAKING THE CHANGE STICK

Transformation versus Transaction

One of the frustrating challenges that we face as leaders is the idea of getting people to embrace the direction that we are trying to take the organization. One of the reasons that people don't embrace the change is that they don't know the "why" of the change. Transformational leadership has an intense focus on why we are doing what we are doing. It has a story to tell and values to back it up. A transaction is simply an exchange though. When there is not a "why" in our messages and there is only what or how, people are not inspired or motivated to change. Never forget what you have learned throughout this book about creating an internal drive in others. Your focus as a super leader has to be on kindling the flame of desire inside the hearts and minds of your people. When you think of creating transformation, you should think about it in terms of starting a movement. You must create clarity of thought in your own mind, because a lack of clarity will always lead to transactional thinking. In the chapter on "leading with clarity," you learned the difference between certainty and clarity. You learned how to look at your interactions with your followers in the right manner. In order to start a movement, you will have to transform the thinking of your team and inspire them to choose the direction you are leading the organization. Most importantly though, you will have to ensure that you have transformed your own thoughts.

The Model For Transforming an Organization

You have a power inside of you that you are likely afraid of. You have a power to change the hearts and minds of others, to influence lasting change. You have a power to change this world, and you have always known that it was there. It is that power that frightens you and excites you at the same time. It is not your weakness that scares you. You are clear on what damage it can do. It is your strength that you fear. It is the leadership prowess that has been caged up inside of your mind and deep within your heart. That caged power for change is lurking in the shadows, waiting for its chance to be released, no, unleashed on the world. You don't know what would happen if you stopped worrying about what others thought of you. There is a part of you that wants to break through the social hypnosis of mediocrity and normalcy. There is a part of you that knows definitely and without reservation, that you have something that this world needs. However, you dredge up the fears of humanity, the fears of not being like everyone else and following the norms. It is that fear, the fear of not being just like everyone else, that has kept your transformational energy caged up. It is the fear of criticism that has prevented the world from understanding and embracing your greatness. But the fear is not real. The fear is manufactured to prevent you from speaking your truth. The turmoil that you feel deep within your psyche is the battle between fear and truth. It is not a battle between good and evil, for those don't exist in this realm. But make no mistake, the battle rages on, and both sides are vying for control of your destiny. The truth that you have always known, but often tried to repress, is the one that will finally set you free! Your truth is the gift that you were designed to give to humanity. It is the positive change that you will offer. That is your truth.

Creating a movement begins with you understanding your definite purpose for which you were made. It is the story of you that must be told in order for you to intentionally become all that you are capable of being. Your fulfillment in life depends on this movement. You will be unhappy, unless you live into your purpose. You learned to identify your values in the beginning of this book, how to create clarity, to define your evolved leadership style, and to develop accountability in yourself and others. You even learned how to become magnetic in your approach to life and leading others. All of those skills and talents are only worthwhile when you employ them for the fulfillment of the truth that exists in you. As you go through this chapter, focus on the steps that are outlined in creating a movement to fulfill your purpose. Focus on who you must be at each step on the journey. It is who you are, not what you do, that will shape the world.

The first step to creating a movement is to unlock your definite purpose. Unlocking this purpose is different than defining it. When someone tries to define their purpose, they are often limited by what others will think of them. They wonder if they will be respected, looked up to, talked down to, or ridiculed. They make their choice about what to pursue in life and what to change, based on their external world. When people do this, they don't own their destiny. It is only when you go deep within yourself, allowing your conscious mind to relax, that you discover your opportunities. If money were off the table and all jobs were compensated equally, what would you do? When you close your eyes and open your mind to the possibilities, what do you see yourself doing? Take a few minutes and simply allow your mind to wander. Allow your thoughts to dance through your head and day dream about what could be. When we unlock the truth of who we are, we unlock the transformation that we were intended to share with the world. Don't think about the world as you do your writing assignment below. Think only of who you have always known you were designed to be. Now, write out your purpose.

I was born to ______________________________________ (activity). I know that by doing this activity every day, I will change my world. It is my potential that I unlock when I live into my purpose. It is the gift that I was always intended to share with the world that lives inside of me.

The second step in creating a movement is …

Overcoming The Resistance

In my opinion, the resistance that exists in this world is the greatest representation of evil. The resistance keeps people from being their best version of themselves. Resistance makes people think that other people have to be just like them. It is the force that manifests conformity and mediocrity. It is what keeps dreams and truth from being. Resistance crushes your soul with the weight of misaligned reality. It is the voice of resistance that tells you that you cannot write a book, you cannot become a chef, you cannot live in another country as a missionary, or you cannot inspire your team to be incredible. It tells you these things, because it knows that you can be. It tells you these things to keep you from becoming the change that the world needs right now, but you will not rest until you have overcome the resistance. You will push through to become the truth that you know, to live into your purpose.

You must create a sense of urgency in the people around you in order to get them to look at the direction you are moving. Without this urgency, they will atrophy in the state they are in right now. You create this urgency through the power of understanding the potential pain of remaining the same and the potential pleasure of moving forward. Most people have no urgency in life, because they are victims of the resistance telling them that they should stay only with what they already know. When you look at the direction that you wish to lead others, what is the pain of remaining just as you are now? Write this out in a statement form to explain what the potential loss is for remaining where you are as an organization or group.

____

____

____

What is the potential gain of moving in this new direction? Write this out in statement form to explain the potential gain for taking action in this new direction.

____

____

____

When the pain of remaining the same is greater than the pain of moving forward, people take action. It is not until the scales are tipped that people begin to move. What motivation are you giving people to enable the scales to tip in the right direction?

____

____

____

The third step in being a transformational leader is to <u>Create An Experience</u> so that you <u>Create A Following</u>. People are hungry for an experience. They wake up in the morning and crave the life that they have envisioned, the one that is exciting and fulfilling. Each of us has had a picture of what we thought life should be like in our minds. We have seen the dreams of doing something great with our lives, of making a difference, of becoming significant. Yet, we spend a very large portion of our life denying the pursuit of this great passion because we are overly concerned with what others might think of us. Knowing that each of us craves an experience with a company and very seldom gets that experience, we become raving fans when we do finally have that desired experience. There are a couple of companies that come to mind when we think about transformational leadership and that transformational change that people are drawn to.

The first company that comes to mind is Starbucks. Yes, Starbucks realized early on that they could not be a powerhouse just selling coffee. So, they stopped selling coffee and began selling their experience. They started as a company that sold coffee beans. They started with a product and tried to compete to sell that product. They understood what they did. Virtually all companies understand the "what" part of their businesses. Thankfully, for all of us that are addicted to the Starbucks experience, they realized that people would pay significantly more for the experience of coffee than they would for the product of coffee. When you walk into a Starbucks, you sense a warm and inviting feel to their stores. They have presented themselves as sophisticated people who understand that you are also a sophisticated person. They have presented themselves as an organization that is fundamentally changing the way that companies employ people, even providing benefits to part time employees. They have presented themselves as a company that inspires you to connect, to be creative, and to take charge of your day by engaging with them. Because they have created an emotional experience, people will pay $4, $5, and even more than that in order to experience their mixed coffees, smoothies, and other consumables. If you simply like coffee, you can make coffee at home. You go to Starbucks, though, to have an experience. Starbucks has a story. They have a story that is compelling and that other people want to be a part of. People want to communicate and be communicated with by being a part of the Starbucks story. Being a part of the story is the key. The integration of the customer into the story is what makes people become raving fans. You become a part of the story when you begin to identify yourself as a "Starbucks" kind of person. You are partaking of the art of coffee with the rest of your Starbucks family.

The second example that quickly comes to mind is the story of Apple. Apple was started and led by a man that truly had a passion for "putting a ding in the universe." Steve Jobs led Apple differently. He wanted to find a way to express his art. He needed to find a way to engage the world in transformation. Jobs began with a tremendous why and an even bigger story. His story of obsessive pursuit of perfection in reshaping the way that people would interact with one another through the use of technology was the driving force behind inspiring his people. He had a big enough vision that people would have to think he was either crazy or a genius. If people are caught off guard enough by the observation, they will often stick around just to see whether the genius is really there. Jobs was theatrical in his presentation of products and brilliant in his pursuit of hype. When his team came up with the iPod, he said that he was creating a musical experience for people that didn't want to carry 10,000 CD's with them, but did want all that music. His objective was to change the way technology integrated into our lives and our lives into technology. Jobs understood that his product was NOT his product. His product, the thing that people would buy, was his presentation. He understood that he had to present the story and the inspiration so that people would buy. They would buy the experience, and the product would be included. He created a flow of information from his soul to the soul of the universe. He did not tell people what to do. He showed them how things could be done. Jobs understood "cool" in the technology world and how it applied to the common person. He was like the techie neighbor who understood your needs and wanted you to simply be happy.

There are a number of other examples of how people created a movement. In every case, though, it takes that one daring person to go against the grain and be willing to be ridiculed. That person is the catalyst for the change. It then takes one brave soul to join the catalyst, so that a spark of innovation and change can take hold. Once you have one true believer, the movement has begun. The catalyst has a responsibility to continue being the example of what all could be, if they simply decided to go in that direction. The believer will then begin to recruit others. They have a desperate need to have made a good decision. The catalyst would have done what they did even if others did not follow. The brave soul needs others to see him or her as right and will, therefore, become evangelical in their building of the following of the catalyst. If you are the catalyst, then find your brave soul by being as intensely passionate about your organization as humanly possible.

The fourth step in being truly transformational is to make it simple to connect with you. This has to do with being able to truly identify with the story that you are buying into. One of the most difficult components of being simple is to come to terms with the fact that your story will not appeal to everyone. There is a group of people that are your target audience. They are people with a common self-definition. It is the way in which they define themselves that makes them naturally drawn to your story. What is fascinating about this portion of being transformational is that it takes real confidence to NOT identify with everyone. Your job is to know who you truly are as a leader. You must know yourself fully, without hiding. By knowing yourself, you can pick up on the characteristics that define you and inspire your team. Once those characteristics are in play, others will take notice and be drawn to you. Southwest Airlines is one of those companies that realized early on that they didn't want to be everything to everyone. Early on, they identified that they couldn't compete just on price. So, Herb Kelleher began looking for ways to connect with people and get them to identify themselves as Southwest Airlines customers and raving fans. Herb liked whiskey and figured out that lots of business people were the same as him. So, when you flew on Southwest in the early days, you got whiskey. You got enough that you had some to take with you to the hotel when you arrived at your destination. Herb understood the power of connection. He understood that there are people that don't like the separation of first class and coach (second class customers). He made people feel valued when they flew with his airline. He made them feel like they were a part of his family. As a result, it was his customers that built his business, not his marketing department. More recently, when airlines began tacking on fees for bags, Southwest used the fact that your first 2 bags fly free as a major way to identify with people. It had very little to do with whether or not you had to pay $25 to bring your bag with you. It had everything to do with the fact that people wanted to be valued and wanted to think that they were doing business with a company that shared their values and their thought patterns. Southwest isn't for everyone. They know that. I have heard stories from people who knew Herb that he would let angry and unhappy passengers know that he would love it if they would fly another airline. A big part of his story was the culture that he built with his team. He defended them. He built them up. He entertained them. Most of all, he made it easy to connect.

The fifth step in being transformational is to exhibit the cool factor. The cool factor is different for different people. It is consistently about you knowing and being able to do something in your area of expertise that excites people. It is about knowing what others wish they knew. It is living how others would love to live but don't think that they will likely every be able to live. Within the training world, trainers look to transformers like Tony Robbins and Zig Ziglar. They see how they pack an arena and how they live the life that others dream about. These are two different examples of living a life of inspired brilliance. With Robbins, it is the complete and total abandonment of fear. It is living a life without limits. It is owning a private island and being able to alter a person's reality in a one-hour session. For Ziglar, it was living a life of inspired significance. It is believing in yourself and in a higher power and in everyone that you encounter. It is waking up every day to the love of your life and being able to make a significant difference in the hearts, minds, and pockets of others. Think about who you look up to. Think about who young people look up to. They see rock stars, movie stars and professional athletes that seem to live larger than life would allow for a common person. They live with an un-commonality that makes us yearn for possibility. They push themselves to be able to accomplish things that others won't, but wish that they could. What is it that you have to offer in the way of being what others aspire to be? What is it that you can do because you have chosen to do that others hope to some day choose as well? When you identify that and join it with the other components of being transformational, others will seek out ways to support your dream. They will support it because deep down, and sometimes not even that deep, the dream that you have is the same dream that they have. You are the living embodiment of the cool that they hope to some day achieve. Be "The Cool."

The final component of being a transformational leader is…

Making The Transformational Connection

You must connect with people at an emotional level first and at a cognitive level second. We don't make our purchases for completely rational reasons. We don't hire or fire people for completely rational reasons either. We don't follow a leader for completely rational reasons. We are, at our core, emotional creatures. We rationalize our emotions, but it is our emotions that drive us to make the choices that we make in life. Emotional resistance is overcome when you connect with people. The majority of this chapter has been about that emotional connection. The other form of connection, and sometimes resistance, is of a cognitive nature. Cognitive, or thought resistance, kicks in when our emotional high about the product, service, or business relationship has subsided. If the emotional response is not great enough, we will begin to use our reasoning mind to work through what we are seeing. Our reasoning mind needs to categorize the experience and filter it through the lens of our past experiences. This apperception (filtering through what we already know) of reality will shape the secondary response of a person as a follower, customer, or partner. From a cognitive standpoint, when we are creating our transformation, we are often fighting what someone else has already done or some other experience that a person has had. We are fighting to get them to unlearn the way in which they have thought in the past. You must give people a reason to follow you after the initial engagement. You have to focus on the results that you are delivering as the justification for engaging with you. There are companies that do incredibly well and are still not great at delivering their product or service. Those companies have told an incredible story though. It is the emotion that is carrying their followership. If you want change to stick and stick for the long term, you have to continuously study what it is that your follower base is looking for. As a leader, you must be able to connect with others through your personal story and then deliver a positive result in their life through your extended interaction. So, the first rule of transforming could be seen as know thyself, or embrace your story. The second could be to connect that part of you that is inspiring to the part of your audience that needs to be inspired. The third component would really be to give the audience as many reason as you can to continue following you. By knowing who they are, what they want, what they need, and how they will define their own success, you are best prepared to deliver something that will guide them and assist them on their journey. From a cognitive vantage point, you must allow your followers to justify following you. Beyond the passion of your story lies the reality of your relationship. Make the relationship solid, the story compelling, and the results positive, and you will never want for followers. They will be pursuing you!

Never forget that leaders are only leaders when others are following. You can only lead a transformation when others desire to follow you. You can only evolve into the highest leadership stage when you are willing to be what others strive to be. Make the choice to be the best version of you each day and strive for each version to be better than the one before. This means that you are in a continuous stage of growth. You will always have the opportunity to be a little better. Accept your chance to grow and pursue opportunities to improve.

The question that I leave you with is the same one that I ask myself every day.

What's next?

Works Cited

All About Steve Jobs Website. (n.d.). *All About Steve Jobs*. Retrieved August 20, 2013, from All About Steve Jobs: http://www.allaboutstevejobs.com

Ecker, T. H. (2005). *Secrets Of The Millionaire Mind.* Harper Business - Harper Collins.

Hill, N. (2012). *Outwitting The Devil.* (S. Lechter, Ed.) New York, NY: Sterling, Reprint Edition.

Hill, N. (1938). *Think And Grow Rich.* Napoleon Hill Foundation.

Jobs, S. (1996). Bitter Steve Jobs Trashes John Sculley. (BBC, Interviewer)

Merriam-Webster Online. (2013). *Merriam Webster Dictionary.* Merriam-Webster Online.

Pressfield, S. (2012). *The War Of Art.* Brooklyn, NY: Black Irish Entertainment, LLC.

Socrates. (n.d.). *Think Exist*. Retrieved August 18, 2013, from Think Exist: http://www.thinkexist.com

Tuckman, B. (1965). *Stages of Group Development.* Columbus, OH: Tuckman.

Tuckman, B. W. (1965). Developmental Sequence in Small Groups. *Psychological Bulletin , 63* (6), pp. 384-399.

Tzu, S. (2007). *The Art of War.* Filiquarian.

Wikipedia. (n.d.). *Wikipedia US*. Retrieved August 20, 2013, from

Wikipedia US:
http://en.wikipedia.org/wiki/Scientific_management

ABOUT THE AUTHOR

Jody Holland is an author, speaker, and entrepreneur. He has started multiple companies over the years, each with the intent of helping organizations achieve more through their people. His big "why" in his life is to create products, services, and tools that assist leaders in bringing out the best in themselves and those that they lead. He does that by continuously studying people and uncovering innovative ways of helping them achieve more and develop others more effectively. He writes books, speaks, trains, and develops tools for leaders. He has spoken for conferences all across the U.S. and abroad. Jody's fun and interactive style of speaking has earned him a reputation in what he calls the "Edu-Tainment" industry. He blends both edu̲c̲a̲t̲i̲o̲n̲ and entertainment together to ensure that people have the highest retention rates possible. Jody has written several other books, including...

25 Activities In A Bag – Team Building Anywhere

My Judo Life – Turning Life's Challenges Into Opportunities

The 12 Principles of Success

Success – A 12 Step Program

Jody blogs regularly at: www.jodynholland.com. If you are interested in booking Jody as a keynote speaker for your next event, you can contact him at: www.LeadershipEvo.com.

Made in the USA
Lexington, KY
23 August 2019